German Doll Marks

and Identification Book

Gold Horse Publishing

Jürgen & Marianne Cieslik

Inquiries should be addressed to:
Gold Horse Publishing,
PO Box 151, Annapolis, Maryland 21404.

Additional copies are available through:
Dollmasters, PO Box 2319, Annapolis, MD 21401
or call 800-966-3655.

Cover Design: David Hirner

$29
ISBN: 1-931503-00-1
Printed in Hong Kong

FOREWORD

"Who made my doll?" "When was it made?" Knowing these facts is important to collectors wishing to make an historical connection or, more pragmatically, simply wishing to place a value on their doll. In identifying the maker of a German doll, there is good news and there is bad news.

The good news is the simple and logical number pattern that most often attaches itself to German dolls. The German registration system, known as D.R.G.M. and begun on October 1, 1891, provided a designer with protection over his designs for a period of three (or six, if renewed) years. This protection inspired doll firms to file registration numbers on each new design or mold; the result for today's collectors is the ability to positively identify and date their dolls from matching the model number or mark on the doll to the number series of a doll firm in the D.R.G.M. series.

The bad news is, simply, that it's not quite that easy. Collectors can be flummoxed in their search by a number of reasons ranging from duplications of a number series to hasty and ill-conceived attributions to simply inaccessibility to identifying the D.R.G.M. series. Doll collecting is, after all, a fairly infantile collecting field. Except for rare examples of European aristocacy or American celebrities few people collected dolls until the 1950's and no really serious attempts at doll identification were begun until the late 1960's. Sadly, even these serious attempts were flawed by hasty conclusions, "wishful thinking", or inaccurate translations. Theory became fact, hypothesis became frozen in stone and collectors became confirmed in faulty thinking that has been difficult to un-do.

During the early 1970's Marianne Cieslik became interested in the history of dolls from her native country of Germany. In studying the available literature two facts became clear: first, that most research was undocumented hypothesis based on randomly confirmed facts that were, dangerously, sometimes right and sometimes wrong; and secondly, that most of the research was done by non-German people, most of whom did not even speak the German language. How, she wondered, could this research be accurate? It was in her quest to confirm - or negate - the conclusions of these researchers that the Ciesliks studies into the German doll industry began.

Unlike any other studies in this field, the Ciesliks works are based upon research and documentation from original sources: D.R.G.M. registation papers, patents, company records, original catalogues and invoices and examination of archive holdings in official museums such as Sonneberg. Their major work on the subject, the German Doll Encyclopedia, 1800-1939, provided the insights from that research to English speaking collectors and will surely remain a classic in the field even as new material continues to be discovered.

Yet the Ciesliks also saw a need for a "ready reference" source book for collectors of German dolls. Such a book could work in unison with the Encyclopedia yet, easily transportable and economical, could be tucked in a hand bag for quick and easy reference. To meet such a need "German Doll Marks and Identification Book" was born. It has been constantly edited and rewritten over the years; this new book is a truly "state of the art" index to knowledge about German doll makers.

All German dolls identified with a model number (not to be confused by the collector with a size number) are listed in numerical order. Reference is then given to the date and number of the D.R.G.M., if available, if not, the collector is given an approximate date of origin based upon research in original company resources. Following is a brief description of the doll as well as possible variations that might occur. Since various companies used identical numbers it is most important to compare doll descriptions in determining which example refers to a particular doll. Also included in the book is a chart of various symbols or logos used by German firms.

This research is on-going and it is the intention of the authors to publish, eventually, a picture volume of each of the model numbers cited. Collectors are invited to participate in the research by advising the authors of additional model numbers or variations which may not be included in this volume.

94.9

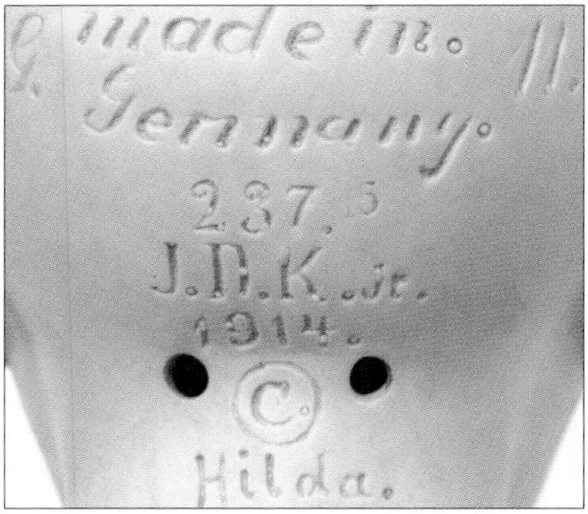
made in
Germany
237.15
J.D.K. Jr.
1914.
C.
Hilda.

79

Heinrich Handwerck

Mold No.	Firm	Date	Description and Identification
12	Theodor Recknage	ca 1912	"RIV", character, solid dome, painted eyes, closed mouth
13	Gebr. Kühnlenz	ca 1885	dolly face, mold number followed by hyphen and size no.
14	Theodor Recknagel	ca 1912	"RIV", character, solid dome, painted eyes, closed mouth, boy
15	Theodor Recknagel	ca 1912	"RIV", character, solid dome, painted eyes, closed mouth, boy
20	Walther & Sohn	ca 1922	"W&S", character, glass eyes, open smiling mouth, sienna Indian
21	Gebr. Kühnlenz	GM 1891	dolly face
22	Theodor Recknagel	GM 1912	character, girl, painted eyes, open/closed laughing mouth, with molded cap with pink or blue bow and ribbon
22	Kämmer & Reinhardt	GM 1912	"K&R", character (see K&R # 122)
23	Theodor Recknagel	GM 1912	character, solid dome, painted eyes, open/closed laughing mouth
24	Theodor Recknagel	GM 1912	character
25	Theodor Recknagel	GM 1912	character, solid dome, painted eye, open/closed laughy mouth, white knit molded cap.
26	Theodor Recknagel	GM 1912	character
27	Theodor Recknagel	GM 1912	character

Mold No.	Firm	Date	Description and Identification
28	Theodor Recknagel	GM 1912	character, boy, painted eyes, open/closed laughing mouth, with molded cap
29	Theodor Recknagel	GM 1912	"RA", character, painted eyes, open/closed laughing mouth, molded cap, with blue ribbon and bow
29	Gebr. Kühnlenz	GM 1891	dolly face
30	Theodor Recknagel	GM 1912	character
30	F&W. Goebel	ca 1890	shoulder head, glass eyes, closed mouth
31	Theodor Recknagel	GM 1912	character, Max, painted googly eyes, closed mouth
31	Unknown	ca 1890	"dep", shoulder head, molded hairs, painted eyes, closed mouth
31	Unknown	ca 1890	"B GERMANY", shoulder head, molded hairs, glass eyes, closed mouth, presumably W.&F. Goebel
32	Theodor Recknagel	GM 1912	character, Moritz, painted googly eyes, closed mouth
32	Gebr. Kühnlenz	ca 1890	dolly face, mold number followed by hyphen and size no.
33	Theodor Recknagel	GM 1914	character
34	Gebr. Kühnlenz	ca 1890	"GK", dolly face, glass eyes, closed mouth
34	C.F. Kling	ca 1885	all bisque, mold number followed by hyphen and size no.

Mold No.	Firm	Date	Description and Identification
34	Theodor Recknagel	GM 1914	character, mold number followed by hyphen and size no., glass eyes, open mouth, Black or Brown doll
34	F&W. Goebel	GM 1887	dolly face
35	Theodor Recknagel	GM 1914	character
37	Theodor Recknagel	GM 1914	character
38	Gebr. Kühnlenz	ca 1890	dolly face, mold number followed by hyphen and size no., shoulder head
39	Theodor Recknagel	GM 1914	character, girl with molded hair, painted eyes, open/closed mouth
40	Max Räder	GM 1910	"dep.", dolly face
41	Theodor Recknagel	GM 1914	character, girl with molded hair, painted googly eyes, open/closed round mouth
41	Gebr. Kühnlenz	ca 1890	dolly face, mold number followed by hyphen and size no.
43	Theodor Recknagel	GM 1914	character, boy with molded cap
44	Theodor Recknagel	GM 1914	character, with painted googly eyes
44	Gebr. Kühnlenz	GM 1895	"dep" or "GK" or "Gebr.K.", dolly face
45	Theodor Recknagel	ca 1914	with and without "RA", character, girl with molded hair, painted googly eyes, closed mouth
46	Theodor Recknagel	ca 1914	character, solid dome, googly eyes, painted pink ribbon
46	F&W. Goebel	GM 1888	dolly face

Mold No.	Firm	Date	Description and Identification
47	Theodor Recknagel	GM 1914	character, painted googly eyes
47	Max Räder	ca 1910	"R-DEP", shoulder head, dolly face
48	Theodor Recknagel	GM 1914	character
49	Theodor Recknagel	GM 1914	"RA", character, Kewpie-type, painted googly eyes, closed mouth
50	Theodor Recknagel	GM 1914	"AR DEP" or "RA", character, Kewpie-type, painted googly eyes, open/closed circular mouth
50	Max Räder	GM 1910	"R.DEP", dolly face, mold number followed by hyphen and size no.
50	F&W. Goebel	ca 1910	""WG"" with crown, character with painted eyes
51	Unknown	ca 1912	character, solid dome with painted hairs, sleep eyes, open mouth
53	Theodor Recknagel	GM 1914	character
54	Theodor Recknagel	GM 1914	character with painted googly eyes
54	F&W. Goebel	GM 1887	presumably dolly face
54	Max Oscar Arnold	ca 1909	"54/14 (Arnoldia)", dolly face
55	Theodor Recknagel	GM 1914	character, solid dome, molded hair, painted eyes, open/closed laughing mouth, upper 2 painted teeth, Black doll
56	Theodor Recknagel	GM 1914	character, solid dome, wide open laughing mouth, painted eyes, baby
56	Gebr. Kühnlenz	ca 1900	dolly face, also with molded moustache as man

Mold No.	Firm	Date	Description and Identification
57	Theodor Recknagel	ca 1912	"RXII", character, solid dome, painted hairs, painted eyes, open/closed mouth (see K&R 100)
58	Theodor Recknagel	GM 1914	character
60	F&W. Goebel	ca 1900	dolly face
62	Gebr. Kühnlenz	ca 1890	dolly face
63	Gebr. Kühnlenz	ca 1890	dolly face
64	Gebr. Kühnlenz	ca 1890	dolly face, shoulder head, glass eyes, closed mouth
68	Gebr. Kühnlenz	GM 1889	dolly face
69	Heinrich Handwerck	ca 1900	dolly face
70	Theodor Recknagel	ca 1912	"R", shoulder head, glass eyes, open mouth
71	Gebr. Kühnlenz	GM 1889	shoulder head, dolly face, mold number followed by hyphen and size no.
72	Gebr. Kühnlenz	GM 1889	dolly face
72	Theodor Recknagel	ca 1912	"RA", solid dome, character, big eyes, grinning closed mouth
73	Theodor Recknagel	ca 1915	grotesque head with big eyes
73	F&W. Goebel	ca 1914	girl head with molded hairs and flowers, painted eyes
75	Gebr. Kühnlenz	GM 1889	dolly face
76	Gebr. Kühnlenz	GM 1889	dolly face

Mold No.	Firm	Date	Description and Identification
77	Gebr. Kühnlenz	GM 1889	dolly face
77	F&W. Goebel	ca 1914	head with molded military cap
77	Seyfarth & Reinhardt	GM 1925	character
79	Heinrich Handwerck	ca 1900	dolly face
79	Schützmeister & Quendt	GM 1891	dolly face
80	Schützmeister & Quendt	GM 1891	"dep", dolly face, sleeping eyes, open mouth
80	F&W. Goebel	ca 1914	character, head, Walter
81	Schützmeister & Quendt	GM 1891	dolly face
82	F&W. Goebel	ca 1914	head with molded German military cap
83	F&W. Goebel	ca 1914	head with molded Austrian military cap
84	F&W. Goebel	ca 1914	"WG", head with molded Bulgarian military cap
85	F&W. Goebel	ca 1914	head with molded Turkey military cap
86	F&W. Goebel	ca 1914	head without cap
86	Theodor Recknagel	ca 1915	character baby
87	F&W. Goebel	ca 1914	head with molded German military cap
88	F&W. Goebel	ca 1914	head with molded Austrian military cap

Mold No.	Firm	Date	Description and Identification
89	F&W. Goebel	ca 1914	head
89	Heinrich Handwerck	ca 1890	dolly face
90	F&W. Goebel	ca 1900	"B/90/185", for Max Handweck, dolly face
91	F&W. Goebel	ca 1914	character
92	F&W. Goebel	GM 1914	character
93	Armand Marseille	GM 1892	"C.O.D." (for Cuno & Otto Dressel), shoulder head (mold number abbreviation for the year 1893)
98	Hertel, Schwab & Co.	ca 1910	"made in Germany", for Koenig & Wernicke, character baby
99	Hertel, Schwab & Co.	ca 1910	"made in Germany", for Koenig & Wernicke, character baby, also as Black doll
99	Heinrich Handwerck	ca 1900	with and without "DEP", dolly face
100	Kämmer & Reinhardt	GM 1909	"K&R", baby, character, solid dome, painted eyes, open/closed mouth, also as Black doll or oriental or with glass eyes and wig
100	Arno Frank	GM 1902	doll head with eye brows made of glass
100	Peter Scherf	GM 1916	character
100	A.Möller & Sohn	ca 1915	"Amuso", dolly face, also as Black doll
100	Unknown	ca 1880	"Elsa", dolly face, solid dome, glass eyes, closed mouth

Mold No.	Firm	Date	Description and Identification
100	Unknown	ca 1920	"made in Germany", character, glass eyes, open nostril, open mouth
101	Kämmer & Reinhardt	GM 1909	"K&R", Peter/Marie, character, painted eyes, closed mouth, rare with glass eyes, also as Black doll
101	Theodor Recknagel	ca 1900	marked with a black head, for L. Bierer, dolly face
101	Peter Scherf	GM 1916	character
101	Schützmeister & Quendt	ca 1900	"SQ", dolly face
101	Adolf Wislizenus	ca 1908	"AW.My Sweetheart B.I.& Co", dolly face, with and without "AW", for B.Illfelder & Co.
101	Unknown	ca 1910	"K", dolly face, sleep eyes, open mouth
101	C.F. Kling	ca 1880	shoulder head, molded hair with painted cap, painted features, molded blouse with painted gold bow
101	Unknown	ca 1900	solid dome, dolly face
102	Kämmer & Reinhardt	GM 1909	"K&R", Elsa/Walter, character, molded hair, painted eyes, closed mouth
102	F&W. Goebel	ca 1912	"G.W" in crown, solid dome, character, glass eyes, closed mouth
102	Peter Scherf	GM 1916	character
103	Schützmeister & Quendt	ca 1900	dolly face

Mold No.	Firm	Date	Description and Identification
103	F&W. Goebel	ca 1910	character, solid dome with painted hair, sleep eyes, closed mouth, boy
103	Kämmer & Reinhardt	ca 1909	"K&R", character, painted eyes, closed mouth
103	Peter Scherf	GM 1916	character
103	Unknown	ca 1890	"X", dolly face, glass eyes, closed mouth
104	Kämmer & Reinhardt	ca 1909	"K&R", character, painted eyes, laughing closed mouth
104	Theodor Recknagel	ca 1915	"RA DEP Germany", character, shoulder head with molded hair, painted eyes, closed mouth
104	Hertwig & Co.	ca 1890	shoulder head with molded flower as hat, painted features
104	Unknown	ca 1880	head, solid dome with 3 holes, painted or glass eyes, closed mouth
105	Kämmer & Reinhardt	ca 1909	"K&R", character, painted eyes, open /closed mouth
105	Theodor Recknagel	ca 1915	"DEP RA", character, shoulder head, solid dome with curly hair, painted eyes, closed mouth
106	Kämmer & Reinhardt	GM 1909	"K&R", character, painted eyes, slightly open /closed mouth
106	F&W. Goebel	ca 1921	presumably character
106	Unknown	ca 1890	dolly face, solid dome, glass eyes, closed mouth
107	Kämmer & Reinhardt	GM 1919	"K&R", Carl, character, painted eyes, closed mouth

Mold No.	Firm	Date	Description and Identification
107	F&W. Goebel	ca 1921	presumably character
108	Kämmer & Reinhardt	ca 1909	character, no further information
109	Kämmer & Reinhardt	GM 1909	"K&R", Elise, character, painted or glass eyes, closed mouth
109	Heinrich Handwerck	ca 1900	dolly face
110	Kämmer & Reinhardt	GM 1909	character, no further information
110	Unknown	ca 1910	character, solid dome, painted eyes, open /closed mouth, for Carl Debes & Sohn, and for Adolf Wislizenus
110	Koenig & Wernicke	ca 1930	"KW Hartgummi Germany", character, flange neck, molded hair
110	F&W. Goebel	ca 1921	presumably character
111	Kämmer & Reinhardt	GM 1909	character, no further information
111	F&W. Goebel	ca 1921	presumably character
111	Unknown	ca 1880	solid dome with 3 holes, glass eyes, closed mouth
112	Kämmer & Reinhardt	GM 1909	"K&R", character, painted or glass eyes, open /closed mouth
113	Unknown	ca 1910	character, painted eyes, open /closed mouth, slightly laughing
114	Kämmer & Reinhardt	GM 1909	"K&R", Hans and Gretchen, character, painted or sleep eyes, closed mouth
114	F&W. Goebel	ca 1921	presumably character

Mold No.	Firm	Date	Description and Identification
114	Porzellanfabrik Rauenstein	ca 1890	china shoulder head with molded hair, painted features.
115	Kämmer & Reinhardt	GM 1911	"S&H/K&R", character, solid dome, sleep eyes, closed mouth
115a	Kämmer & Reinhardt	GM 1911	"S&H/K&R", character, sleep eyes, closed mouth, wig
116	Kämmer & Reinhardt	GM 1911	"S&H/K&R", character, solid dome, sleep eyes, open /closed mouth
116	C.F. Kling	ca 1880	shoulder head with molded hair and hat, glass eyes, closed mouth
116a	Kämmer & Reinhardt	GM 1911	"S&H/K&R", character, sleep eyes, open/closed mouth or with open mouth, wig, also as Black doll
117	Kämmer & Reinhardt	GM 1911	"S&H/K&R My Darling", character, glass eyes, closed mouth, rare with open mouth, "My Sweet Darling"
117a	Kämmer & Reinhardt	GM 1911	"S&H/K&R", character, glass eyes, closed mouth
117x	Kämmer & Reinhardt	GM 1911	"S&H/K&R", character, presumably lower size no. of mold number 117
117n	Kämmer & Reinhardt	GM 1916	"S&H/K&R My New Darling, character, sleep eyes, open mouth, "My New Darling"
118	Kämmer & Reinhardt	ca 1911	"S&H/K&R", character, sleep eyes, open mouth

Mold No.	Firm	Date	Description and Identification
118a	Kämmer & Reinhardt	ca 1911	"S&H/K&R", character, sleep eyes, open mouth
118	Unknown	ca 1890	shoulder head, glass eyes, open mouth, dolly face, presumably Kestner
119	Kämmer & Reinhardt	ca 1913	"S&H/K&R", baby, character, sleep eyes, open /closed mouth
119	Heinrich Handwerck	ca 1900	dolly face
119	C.F. Kling	ca 1880	shoulder head with molded hair, glass eyes, closed mouth.
120	Kämmer & Reinhardt	ca 1915	"S&H", character, sleep eyes, open mouth
120	F&W. Goebel	ca 1921	character, sleep eyes, open mouth
120	Max Friedr. Schelhorn	GM 1912	character, multi-face
120	J.D. Kestner jr.	GM 1897	dolly face
120	Otto Gans	ca 1910	"OG", dolly face
121	Kämmer & Reinhardt	GM 1912	"K&R", character, sleep eyes, open mouth, "My Little Darling"
121	F&W. Goebel	ca 1921	presumably character
121	Max Friedr. Schelhorn	GM 1912	character, multi-face
121	Theodor Recknagel	ca 1905	head, dolly face
121	Unknown	ca 1900	marked with crown, dolly face
121	Unknown	ca 1880	head, solid dome with 3 holes, closed mouth

Mold No.	Firm	Date	Description and Identification
121	J.D. Kestner jr.	GM 1897	dolly face
121	Unknown	ca 1910	clown with molded cap, painted features
121	Nikolaus Oberender	ca 1920	"NO", dolly face
122	Kämmer & Reinhardt	GM 1912	"S&H/K&R", character, sleep eyes, open mouth,also with "P Germany"
122	Max Friedr. Schelhorn	GM 1912	character, multi-face
122	F&W. Goebel	ca 1921	presumably character
122	C.F. Kling	GM 1881	shoulder head with molded hair, glass eyes, closed mouth
122	Unknown	ca 1900	"M", dolly face
122	J.D. Kestner jr.	GM 1897	dolly face
123	Kämmer & Reinhardt	GM 1913	"S&H/K&R", character, Max, flirting sleep eyes, laughing closed mouth
123	Max Friedr. Schelhorn	GM 1912	character, multi-face
123	F&W. Goebel	ca 1921	presumably character
123	C.F. Kling	ca 1880	with bell, shoulder head, glass eyes, open or closed mouth
123	J.D. Kestner jr.	GM 1897	dolly face
124	Kämmer & Reinhardt	GM 1913	"S&H/K&R", character, Moritz, flirting sleep eyes, laughing closed mouth

Mold No.	Firm	Date	Description and Identification
124	F&W. Goebel	ca 1921	presumably character
124	C.F. Kling	ca 1880	with bell, shoulder head, sleep eyes, open mouth
124	Unknown	ca 1900	"WD" with crown, dolly face
124	J.D. Kestner jr.	GM 1897	dolly face
125	Kämmer & Reinhardt	ca 1914	character, no further information
125	Unknown	ca 1914	character, sleep eyes, smiling mouth, presumably K&R
125	F&W. Goebel	ca 1921	presumably character
125	Unknown	ca 1930	"Germany", character, solid dome, painted hair, glass eyes, open /closed mouth
125	Nikolaus Oberender	ca 1910	"NO", character, sleep eyes, open mouth
125	Unknown	ca 1890	shoulder head, china, molded hair, painted features
125	J.D. Kestner jr.	GM 1897	dolly face
125	C.F. Kling	ca 1890	with bell, shoulder head, molded blonde hair, painted features
126	Kämmer & Reinhardt	ca 1914	"S&H/K&R", My Darling baby, character, sleeping or flirting eyes or all-bisque- baby (body marked with "1126-19", "My Darling baby"
126	Hertel, Schwab & Co.	ca 1928	character, solid dome with painted hair, sleep eyes, open mouth, Skippy

Mold No.	Firm	Date	Description and Identification
126	Eisenmann & Co.	GM 1913	character
126	F&W. Goebel	ca 1921	presumably character
126	Walther & Sohn	ca 1920	character, head
126	Theodor Recknagel	ca 1925	newborn, flange neck, sleep eyes, closed mouth
126	J.D. Kestner jr.	GM 1897	dolly face
127	Kämmer & Reinhardt	GM 1914	"K&R", character, solid dome, sleep eyes, open mouth (see mold 126)
127	Hertel, Schwab & Co.	ca 1928	character, solid dome with molded hair, sleep eyes, open mouth, Patsy
127	Hertel, Schwab & Co. (presumably)	ca 1915	character, solid dome with painted eyes, open /closed and smiling mouth
127	Theodor Recknagel	ca 1925	newborn, flange neck, sleep eyes, closed mouth, Black doll
127	J.D. Kestner jr.	GM 1897	dolly face
128	Kämmer & Reinhardt	GM 1914	character, sleep eyes, open mouth
128	Hermann Steiner	ca 1920	"HS", character
128	C.F. Kling	ca 1880	shoulder head with molded hair and black comb, glass eyes, closed mouth
128	Unknown	ca 1910	character, glass eyes, closed mouth
128	Theodor Recknagel	GM 1925	head with one tooth

Mold No.	Firm	Date	Description and Identification
128	J.D. Kestner jr.	GM 1897	dolly face, glass eyes, closed mouth
129	Hertel, Schwab & Co.	ca 1910	"made in Germany", character, sleep eyes, closed mouth
129	Sonneberger Porzellanfabrik	ca 1900	"SP", dolly face
129	C.F. Kling	ca 1880	shoulder head, china or bisque, with molded hair, painted eyes, closed mouth
129	Theodor Recknagel	GM 1925	head with 2 teeth
129	J.D. Kestner jr.	GM 1897	dolly face
129	Unknown	ca 1910	solid dome, grotesque features, glass eyes, laughing closed mouth, with and without clown painting
130	Wiesenthal, Schindel & Kallenberg	ca 1912	"WSK", character, painted eyes, open /closed mouth
130	Max Oscar Arnold	ca 1920	"MOA", character
130	Hertel, Schwab & Co.	ca 1912	character, sleep eyes, open /closed mouth
130	C.F. Kling	ca 1885	with bell, shoulder head, glass eyes, closed mouth
130	J.D. Kestner jr.	ca 1897	dolly face
131	Kämmer & Reinhardt	ca 1914	"S&H/K&R", character, googly eyes, closed mouth

Mold No.	Firm	Date	Description and Identification
131	C.F. Kling	ca 1885	with bell or mold number, china shoulder head with molded hair, painted features, or bisque with molded hair, glass eyes, closed mouth
131	Hertel, Schwab & Co.	ca 1912	character, solid dome, painted eyes, closed mouth
131	Theodor Recknagel	GM 1926	head
131	J.D. Kestner jr.	GM 1897	dolly face
132	Kämmer & Reinhardt	GM 1921	character
132	Hertel, Schwab & Co.	ca 1912	"made in Germany", character, sleep eyes, open mouth with tongue
132	Theodor Recknagel	GM 1926	head
132	J.D. Kestner jr.	GM 1897	dolly face
133	Kämmer & Reinhardt	GM 1923	character
133	Hermann Steiner	ca 1920	"HS", character, googly eyes, closed mouth
133	Hugo Wiegand	ca 1920	"HW", character, head
133	Hertel, Schwab & Co.	ca 1912	character, solid dome, painted eyes, closed mouth, for Kley & Hahn
133	C.F. Kling	ca 1885	shoulder head with molded hair, glass eyes, closed mouth
133	J.D. Kestner jr.	GM 1897	dolly face

Mold No.	Firm	Date	Description and Identification
133	Gebr. Kühnlenz	ca 1900	"GbrK" in sun, dolly face
133	Keramisches Werk	ca 1932	"KWG", character, composition, sleep eyes, open mouth
134	Keramisches Werk	ca 1932	"KWG", character, composition, also as Black doll
134	Hermann Steiner	ca 1920	"HS", Black doll
134	Hertel, Schwab & Co.	ca 1915	character, sleep eyes, closed mouth
134	Theodor Recknagel	GM 1926	head
134	C.F. Kling	ca 1890	dolly face, molded hair with hat, painted features
134	J.D. Kestner jr.	GM 1897	dolly face
135	Kämmer & Reinhardt	ca 1923	character, sleep eyes, open mouth
135	Hertel, Schwab & Co.	ca 1912	character, solid dome, painted eyes, open /closed mouth, for Kley & Hahn
135	Theodor Recknagel	GM 1926	baby
135	C.F. Kling	ca 1885	shoulder head, molded hair, molded blouse, painted eyes, closed mouth, also with molded flowers and glass eyes
135	J.D. Kestner jr.	GM 1897	dolly face
136	Hertel, Schwab & Co.	ca 1912	"made in Germany", character, sleep eyes, open mouth

Mold No.	Firm	Date	Description and Identification
136	Keramisches Werk	ca 1932	"KWG", character, composition
136	Unknown	ca 1905	glass eyes, closed mouth
136	Theodor Recknagel	GM 1926	baby
136	J.D. Kestner jr.	GM 1897	dolly face, glass eyes, closed mouth
137	Theodor Recknagel	ca 1925	newborn, flange neck, sleep eyes, closed mouth
137	J.D. Kestner jr.	GM 1897	dolly face, solid dome, glass eyes, closed mouth
137	Keramisches Werk	ca 1932	"KWG", character, baby, composition
137	Unknown	ca 1890	dolly face, glass eyes, closed mouth
138	Hertel, Schwab & Co.	ca 1912	"K&H", character, solid dome, painted or sleep eyes, open /closed mouth with molded tongue, for Kley & Hahn
138	Theodor Recknagel	ca 1925	"RA", newborn, flange neck or head, sleep eyes, closed mouth, also as Black doll
138	Unknown	ca 1890	dolly face, glass eyes, closed mouth
138	J.D. Kestner jr.	GM 1897	dolly face
139	Heinrich Handwerck	ca 1900	dolly face
139	J.D. Kestner jr.	ca 1897	dolly face

Mold No.	Firm	Date	Description and Identification
140	Hertel, Schwab & Co.	ca 1912	character, glass eyes, open /closed mouth, laughing
140	C.F. Kling	ca 1885	shoulder head, molded hair, boy, painted or glass eyes, closed mouth
140	Unknown	ca 1890	shoulder head with molded porcelain pate over which the wig is attached, glass eyes, closed mouth
140	J.D. Kestner jr.	GM 1897	dolly face
140	Heinr. Handwerck	ca 1900	"Handwerck's Imperial", shoulder head, dolly face
141	Theodor Recknagel	ca 1925	"RA", solid dome, sleep eyes, closed mouth, newborn
141	Hertel, Schwab & Co.	ca 1912	character, painted or glass eyes, open /closed mouth with molded tongue
142	C.F. Kling	GM 1881	doll head
142	J.D. Kestner jr.	GM 1897	dolly face
142	Kämmer & Reinhardt	ca 1923	"S&H/K&R", character baby, sleep eyes, open mouth
142	Hertel, Schwab & Co.	ca 1912	character, solid dome, painted or sleep eyes, open /closed mouth or open mouth with molded tongue
142	Geo. Borgfeldt & Co.	GM 1925	crawling baby with character head
142	C.F. Kling	GM 1881	doll head

Mold No.	Firm	Date	Description and Identification
142	J.D. Kestner jr.	GM 1897	dolly face
143	Hertel, Schwab & Co.	ca 1912	character, glass eyes, closed smiling mouth with molded teeth
143	J.D. Kestner jr.	GM 1897	dolly face, glass eyes, open mouth
143	C.F. Kling	ca 1881	shoulder head, molded, painted hair, painted eyes, closed mouth
144	Kämmer & Reinhardt	ca 1920	"K&R", character, painted eyes, closed mouth
144	J.D. Kestner jr.	GM 1897	dolly face
144	Koenig & Wernicke	ca 1935	character, sleep eyes, open mouth, composition
145	J.D. Kestner jr.	GM 1897	dolly face
146	J.D. Kestner jr.	GM 1897	dolly face
147	Hertel, Schwab & Co.	ca 1914	character, googly eyes, open /closed mouth
147	J.D. Kestner jr.	ca 1897	shoulder head, dolly face
148	Hertel, Schwab & Co.	ca 1910	character, glass eyes, open /closed mouth, crying with real tears
148	C.F. Kling	ca 1885	"bell", shoulder head, molded hair, painted eyes, closed mouth
148	J.D. Kestner jr.	ca 1897	shoulder head, dolly face
149	Hertel, Schwab & Co.	ca 1912	character, sleep or painted eyes, closed mouth

Mold No.	Firm	Date	Description and Identification
149	J.D. Kestner jr.	ca 1897	dolly face
149	C.F. Kling	ca 1885	"bell", shoulder head with molded hair, china, painted face
150	Hertel, Schwab & Co.	ca 1912	character, solid dome or with wig, painted or sleep eyes, open /closed or open mouth with tongue
150	Hertel, Schwab & Co.	ca 1911	"WSK-DRGM -452711", character, sleep eyes, open /closed mouth, for Wiesenthal, Schindel & Kallenberg
150	Simon & Halbig	ca 1912	character, painted eyes, closed mouth
150	Max Oscar Arnold	ca 1920	"MOA-Welsch", character, for Welsch & Co.
150	Gebr. Ohlhaver	ca 1920	character
150	J.D. Kestner jr.	ca 1897	dolly face
151	Hertel, Schwab & Co.	ca 1912	with and without "made in Germany", character, solid dome, painted or sleep eyes, open or open /closed mouth, molded tongue
151	Hertel, Schwab & Co.	ca 1912	same as before, but with "2046"
151	Simon & Halbig	ca 1912	"S&H", character, painted eyes, open /closed mouth, laughing with molded teeth
151	Gebr. Ohlhaver	ca 1920	triangle with sun and eye, shoulder head, character

Mold No.	Firm	Date	Description and Identification
151	C.F. Kling	ca 1885	shoulder head with molded hair and molded blouse, glass eyes, closed mouth
151	J.D. Kestner jr.	ca 1897	dolly face
152	Hertel, Schwab & Co.	ca 1912	character, sleep eyes, open mouth
152	Hertel, Schwab & Co.	ca 1912	same as before, only with "LW&Co.", for Louis Wolf & Co.
152	Simon & Halbig	ca 1912	character, painted eyes, closed mouth
152	J.D. Kestner jr.	ca 1897	dolly face
152	C.F.Kling	ca 1885	shoulder head, glass eyes, open /closed mouth
153	Simon & Halbig	ca 1912	character, molded hair, painted eyes, closed mouth, boy
153	J.D. Kestner jr.	ca 1887	dolly face, solid dome with 2 holes, glass eyes, closed mouth
153	C.F. Kling	ca 1885	shoulder head, molded hair, glass eyes, closed mouth
154	Hertel, Schwab & Co.	ca 1912	character, solid dome, glass eyes, closed mouth, for Kley & Hahn
154	Unknown	ca 1895	dolly face, solid dome, glass eyes, closed mouth
154	J.D. Kestner jr.	ca 1897	"dep", shoulder head, dolly face, also as Black doll
154	C.F. Kling	ca 1885	shoulder head, molded hair, glass eyes, closed mouth

Mold No.	Firm	Date	Description and Identification
155	J.D. Kestner jr.	ca 1897	dolly face, glass eyes, open mouth, also as Oriental
155	Hertel, Schwab & Co.	ca 1912	"K&W", character, glass eyes, open mouth, for Koenig & Wernicke
155	Unknown	ca 1900	dolly face, sleep eyes, open mouth, Black doll
156	Simon & Halbig	GM 1926	"AHW", character, sleep eyes, open mouth, for Adolf Hülss, also in celluloid
156	C.F. Kling	ca 1885	shoulder head, molded hair, painted eyes, closed mouth
156	J.D. Kestner jr.	GM 1898	dolly face
156	Franz Schmidt & Co.	ca 1930	"F.S.&Co.", character, sleep eyes, open mouth, composition
157	C.F. Kling	ca 1895	dolly face, shoulder head, glass eyes, closed mouth, boy
157	Simon & Halbig	GM 1927	"AHW", character, for Adolf Hülls
157	Hertel, Schwab & Co.	ca 1912	character, sleep eyes, closed mouth
157	Unknown	ca 1900	glass eyes, laughing closed mouth with molded teeth, clown
158	Hertel, Schwab & Co.	ca 1911	"K&H", character, painted or glass eyes, open mouth, for Kley & Hahn
159	Hertel, Schwab & Co.	GM 1911	2-face-doll, crying and laughing, also separate heads laughing and crying possible, painted eyes, open /closed mouth, for Kley & Hahn

Mold No.	Firm	Date	Description and Identification
159	Simon & Halbig	ca 1911	character
159	J.D. Kestner jr.	ca 1898	dolly face, shoulder head
159	Koenig & Wernicke	ca 1920	"KWW", character, sleep eyes, open mouth
160	Simon & Halbig	ca 1914	"H.H.-S&H", character, sleep eyes, open mouth, for Heinrich Handwerck
160	Hertel, Schwab & Co.	ca 1912	"K&H", character, sleep eyes, open /closed mouth, for Kley & Hahn
160	Koenig & Wernicke	ca 1930	"K&W", character, composition
160	C.F. Kling	ca 1885	shoulder head with molded hair and hat, glass eyes, closed mouth, molded blouse
160	J.D. Kestner jr.	ca 1898	dolly face
161	Hertel, Schwab & Co.	ca 1912	character, sleep eyes, open /closed mouth, for Kley & Hahn
161	J.D. Kestner jr.	ca 1898	dolly face
162	Hertel, Schwab & Co.	ca 1912	character, sleep eyes, open mouth, with cut out for voice, for Kley & Hahn
162	Unknown	ca 1920	character, googly eyes, open /closed laughing mouth
162	J.D. Kestner jr.	ca 1898	dolly face
162	C.F. Kling	ca 1890	shoulder head, glass eyes, closed mouth

Mold No.	Firm	Date	Description and Identification
163	Hertel, Schwab & Co.	ca 1914	character, molded bobbed hair, googly eyes, closed smiling mouth, Jubilee-Doll, for Strobel & Wilken
163	Unknown	ca 1912	character, solid dome, molded hair, painted eyes, closed mouth
163	J.D. Kestner jr.	ca 1898	shoulder head, glass eyes, closed mouth, "Gibson Girl"
164	Simon & Halbig	ca 1912	with and without "S&H", head, glass eyes, open mouth, Oriental
164	J.D. Kestner jr.	ca 1898	dolly face
164	Hertel, Schwab & Co.	ca 1914	character, googly sleep eyes, smiling closed mouth
165	Hertel, Schwab & Co.	ca 1914	character, googly eyes, smiling closed mouth
165	Gebr. Kühnlenz	ca 1900	"Gbr.K.", dolly face
166	C.F. Kling	ca 1885	dolly face, shoulder head, glass eyes, closed mouth
166	Hertel, Schwab & Co.	ca 1912	"K&H", character, solid dome, with painted hair, sleep eyes, closed or open mouth, for Kley & Hahn, boy
166	J.D. Kestner jr.	GM 1898	dolly face, shoulder head
167	Hertel, Schwab & Co.	ca 1912	"K&H", character, sleep eyes, open /closed or open mouth, for Kley & Hahn
167	C.F. Kling	ca 1885	with bell, shoulder head, solid dome with wig, closed or open mouth

Mold No.	Firm	Date	Description and Identification
167	J.D. Kestner jr.	ca 1898	dolly face
168	J.D. Kestner jr.	ca 1898	dolly face
168	Simon & Halbig	ca 1915	"AHW Germany" in circle, sleep eyes, open mouth, for Adolf Hülss
169	Hertel, Schwab & Co.	ca 1912	"K&H", character, sleep eyes, with closed or open /closed mouth, for Kley & Hahn
169	Porzellanfabrik Burggrub	ca 1930	character
169	Unknown	ca 1910	"Special", glass eyes, open mouth
169	J.D. Kestner jr.	ca 1898	dolly face, glass eyes, closed mouth
170	C.F. Kling	ca 1885	shoulder head with molded hair and bow, glass eyes, closed mouth, molded blouse
170	Kämmer & Reinhardt	GM 1925	solid dome, newborn, flange neck, sleep eyes, open mouth, also with mold number 8170
170	Hertel, Schwab & Co.	ca 1915	"K&W", character, sleep eyes, laughing , open mouth, for König & Wernicke
170	Porzellanfabrik Burggrub	ca 1930	"SHPB", character, sleep eyes, open mouth
170	Geo. Borgfeldt & Co.	GM 1927	character
170	Simon & Halbig	GM 1911	presumably character
170	J.D. Kestner jr.	ca 1903	dolly face
170	Gebr. Kühnlenz	ca 1910	"GbrK", shoulder head, dolly face

Mold No.	Firm	Date	Description and Identification
171	Kämmer & Reinhardt	GM 1925	solid dome, newborn, flange neck, sleep eyes, open mouth, also with mold number 8171, Klein-Mammy
171	Unknown	ca 1910	dolly face
171	Simon & Halbig	GM 1911	presumably character
171	J.D. Kestner jr.	ca 1900	dolly face
172	Hertel, Schwab & Co.	ca 1914	solid dome, googly eyes, smiling, closed mouth, Jubilee-Doll, for Strobel & Wilken
172	Simon & Halbig	GM 1911	presumably character
172	J.D. Kestner jr.	ca 1900	shoulder head, glass eyes, closed mouth, Gibson Girl
172	C.F. Kling	ca 1890	dolly face, shoulder head, glass eyes, closed mouth
172	Kämmer & Reinhardt	GM 1925	"P S&H" or "P III", solid dome, newborn, flange neck, sleep eyes, closed mouth, also with mold number 8172
173	Kämmer & Reinhardt	GM 1925	"K&R S&H", solid dome, newborn, flange neck, sleep eyes, open mouth, also with mold number 8173
173	Hertel, Schwab & Co.	ca 1914	character, solid dome or with wig, googly, smiling/closed mouth, Jubilee Doll, for Strobel & Wilken
173	Simon & Halbig	GM 1911	presumably character
174	Unknown	ca 1912	"LH", character, solid dome, open /closed mouth

Mold No.	Firm	Date	Description and Identification
174	Simon & Halbig	GM 1911	"Superior", character, for Heinrich Handwerck
174	J.D. Kestner jr.	ca 1905	dolly face
175	Kämmer & Reinhardt	GM 1928	solid dome, newborn, flange neck, also with der mold number 8175, Little Mommy
175	Hertel, Schwab & Co.	ca 1914	solid dome, the Winker, closed laughing mouth
175	Hertwig & Co.	GM 1916	
175	Simon & Halbig	GM 1911	presumably character
176	Hertel, Schwab & Co.	ca 1912	"K&H", character, sleep eyes, open mouth with movable tongue, for Kley & Hahn
176	Simon & Halbig	ca 1925	"S&H" or "AHW 101", character, sleep eyes, open mouth, with "AHW" for Adolf Hülss
176	Carl Beck & Alfred Schulze	ca 1925	character, newborn
176	C.F. Kling	ca 1885	shoulder head, china or bisque, painted features
177	C.F. Kling	ca 1885	shoulder head, molded hair, painted eyes, closed mouth, lady
177	Unknown	ca 1920	character, painted eyes, open /closed mouth
178	Hertel, Schwab & Co.	ca 1915	character, solid dome, molded hair, googly eyes, open mouth, for Kley & Hahn

Mold No.	Firm	Date	Description and Identification
178	C.F. Kling	ca 1885	shoulder head, molded hair, glass eyes, closed mouth
178	J.D. Kestner jr.	ca 1909	character, painted eyes, open /closed mouth
179	Hertel, Schwab & Co.	ca 1915	"K&W", character, for Koenig & Wernicke
179	Unknown	ca 1925	"Butler", character, googly eyes, closed mouth
179	J.D. Kestner jr.	ca 1909	character, painted or glass eyes, open or open /closed mouth
180	Hertel, Schwab & Co.	ca 1915	"K&W", character, googly eyes, laughing , open /closed mouth, for Kley & Hahn
180	J.D. Kestner jr.	ca 1910	character, painted eyes, open /closed mouth or with sleep eyes and fur brows
180	C.F. Kling	ca 1885	shoulder head, molded hair with black bow, painted features
180	Unknown	ca 1890	"XIII", dolly face, solid dome, glass eyes, closed mouth
181	Hertel, Schwab & Co.	ca 1915	character, sleep eyes, open mouth
181	Gebr. Knoch	ca 1900	dolly face
181	J.D. Kestner jr.	ca 1910	character, painted eyes, open /closed mouth
181	Unknown	ca 1890	shoulder head, solid dome, glass eyes, closed mouth

Mold No.	Firm	Date	Description and Identification
182	C.F. Kling	ca 1885	shoulder head, molded hair, painted or glass eyes, closed mouth or with wig and open mouth
182	J.D. Kestner jr.	ca 1910	character, painted or glass eyes, closed mouth
182	Unknown	ca 1890	solid dome, glass eyes, closed mouth
182	Unknown	ca 1925	"Germany 62", dolly face with blushed cheek
182	Hertel, Schwab & Co.	ca 1915	character, sleep eyes, open mouth
183	J.D. Kestner jr.	ca 1910	character, glass eyes, open /closed mouth with molded teeth
183	Unknown	ca 1890	solid dome, glass eyes, closed mouth
184	J.D. Kestner jr.	ca 1910	character, painted or glass eyes, closed mouth
185	Gebr. Knoch	ca 1900	"GKN", dolly face
185	F&W. Goebel	ca 1900	"Bebe Elite", dolly face for Max Handwerck
185	C.F. Kling	ca 1885	shoulder head, molded hair, painted eyes, closed mouth
185	J.D. Kestner jr.	ca 1910	character, painted or glass eyes, open /closed mouth
186	C.F. Kling	ca 1885	"bell", shoulder head, molded hair, painted or glass eyes, closed mouth

Mold No.	Firm	Date	Description and Identification
186	J.D. Kestner jr.	ca 1910	character, painted eyes, open /closed mouth with molded teeth
187	J.D. Kestner jr.	ca 1910	character, painted eyes, open /closed mouth with molded teeth
188	C.F. Kling	ca 1885	"bell", shoulder head, molded hair, glass eyes, closed mouth or china with painted features
189	Heinrich Handwerck	ca 1900	dolly face
189	Gebr. Knoch	ca 1900	"GKN", dolly face
189	J.D. Kestner jr.	ca 1910	character, glass eyes, closed mouth
189	C.F. Kling	ca 1885	with bell, shoulder head, china, molded hair, painted features or in bisque with glass eyes and closed mouth
190	Gebr. Knoch	ca 1900	"GKN", dolly face
190	Unknown	ca 1900	shoulder head, dolly face
190	C.F. Kling	ca 1885	shoulder head, molded hair, painted or glass eyes closed mouth
190	J.D. Kestner jr.	ca 1910	character, painted eyes, open /closed mouth
191	Kämmer & Reinhardt	ca 1900	with and without "K&R", dolly face
191	Porzellanfabrik Rauenstein	ca 1895	"Alice", dolly face
191	J.D. Kestner jr.	ca 1910	character, glass eyes, open /closed mouth

Mold No.	Firm	Date	Description and Identification
192	Kämmer & Reinhardt	ca 1900	with and without "K&R", dolly face with closed or open mouth
192	Gebr. Knoch	ca 1900	"GKN", dolly face
192	J.D. Kestner jr.	GM 1910	presumably character with or without glass eyes
193	Gebr. Knoch	ca 1900	"GKN", dolly face
195	J.D. Kestner jr.	ca 1910	"Dep made in Germany", shoulder head, fur brows, dolly face
196	J.D. Kestner jr.	ca 1910	head, fur brows, dolly face
199	Heinrich Handwerck	ca 1900	dolly face
199	Unknown	ca 1915	"Germany", character, sleep eyes, open mouth
199	J.D. Kestner jr.	ca 1910	shoulder head or head, dolly face
199	Gebr. Knoch	ca 1900	"GKN made in Germany DEP", dolly face
200	Kämmer & Reinhardt	ca 1909	character, shoulder head, painted eyes, open /closed mouth (see mold # 100)
200	Armand Marseille	GM 1911	"AM 243", character, googly eyes, closed mouth with molded tongue
200	Catterfelder Puppenfabrik	GM 1910	"CP", character, solid dome, painted eyes, open /closed mouth
200	Walther & Sohn	ca 1922	"W&S", character, googly eyes, closed mouth

Mold No.	Firm	Date	Description and Identification
200	Gebr. Heubach	ca 1915	with square, "W.u.Z.I.", dolly face, shoulder head, for Wagner & Zetsche, on the headcrown "10556"
200	J.D. Kestner jr.	ca 1908	dolly face, shoulder head, celluloid (turtle-mark)
200	C.F. Kling	ca 1895	with bell, shoulder head china or in bisque, molded hair, painted eyes, closed mouth
200	Hertel, Schwab & Co.	ca 1912	"L.W.&Co", character, shoulder head, solid dome, laughing, for Louis Wolf & Co.
200	Max Oscar Arnold	ca 1920	"MOA-Welsch", dolly face, for Welsch & Co.
201	Kämmer & Reinhardt	GM 1909	character, shoulder head, painted eyes, closed mouth, (Peter and Marie), (see mold # 101)
201	Catterfelder Puppenfabrik	ca 1910	"CP", character, solid dome, painted eyes, open /closed mouth
201	Baehr & Proeschild	ca 1888	"DEP", dolly face
201	Gebr. Knoch	ca 1900	"GKN made in Germany DEP", dolly face, white or Black doll
201	Schützmeister & Quendt	ca 1920	"SQ", character, baby, sleep eyes, open mouth
201	Fritz Dressel	GM 1926	"Dreso-doll"
201	Unknown	ca 1920	"Gy", character, sleep eyes, open mouth
201	J.D. Kestner jr.	ca 1908	dolly face, shoulder head, celluloid (turtle-mark)

Mold No.	Firm	Date	Description and Identification
202	Simon & Halbig	GM 1887	"DEP", multi-face-doll white or black
202	C.F. Kling	ca 1890	shoulder head, china, molded hair, painted features
202	Fritz Dressel	GM 1926	"Dreso-doll"
203	Gebr. Knoch	ca 1910	character, shoulder head, painted eyes, closed mouth
203	Fritz Dressel	GM 1926	"Dreso-doll"
203	C.F. Kling	ca 1890	shoulder head, molded hair, glass eyes, closed mouth
203	J.D. Kestner jr.	ca 1920	"JDK" with turtle-mark, character, sleep eyes, open mouth, celluloid
203	Unknown	ca 1915	character, sleep eyes, open /closed mouth
204	Baehr & Proeschild	ca 1888	head, glass eyes, closed mouth
204	Gebr. Knoch	ca 1910	character
204	Schützmeister & Quendt	ca 1920	"SQ", character, baby
205	Armand Marseille	ca 1918	"AM", character, baby
205	Catterfelder Puppenfabrik	GM 1909	character
205	Gebr. Knoch	ca 1910	"GKN", character, shoulder head, painted eyes, open /closed mouth, molded tongue
206	Catterfelder Puppenfabrik	GM 1909	character

Mold No.	Firm	Date	Description and Identification
206	J.D. Kestner jr.	ca 1910	character, sleep eyes, closed mouth
206	Gebr. Knoch	ca 1910	"Made in Germany DRGM ", character, solid dome, painted eyes, open /closed laughing mouth, also as Black doll
207	Baehr & Proeschild	ca 1888	dolly face, glass eyes, closed mouth
207	Catterfelder Puppenfabrik	ca 1910	character, painted eyes, closed mouth
207	Adolf Greuling	GM 1897	Harlekin
207	Schützmeister & Quendt	ca 1925	"SQ", character, sleep eyes, open mouth
208	Catterfelder Puppenfabrik	ca 1910	"CP deponiert", character, with solid dome or wig, painted or sleep eyes, open mouth, movable tongue
208	Gebr. Knoch	ca 1910	"GKN", character, shoulder head
208	Walther & Sohn	ca 1920	character, googly eyes, closed mouth
208	J.D. Kestner jr.	ca 1910	"Made in Germany", character, painted or glass eyes, closed smiling mouth with molded teeth
208	Baehr & Proeschild	ca 1885	dolly face, glass eyes, closed mouth
209	Baehr & Proeschild	ca 1888	with and without "Germany", glass eyes, open mouth, dolly face
209	Catterfelder Puppenfabrik	ca 1910	"CP", character, sleep eyes, open mouth with movable tongue

Mold No.	Firm	Date	Description and Identification
210	Armand Marseille	GM 1911	"AM 243", character, solid dome, painted googly eyes, closed mouth
210	Richard Scherzer	GM 1926	newborn (a 3 day old baby)
210	Fritz Dressel	GM 1926	"Dreso-doll"
210	Theodor Wendt (presumably)	ca 1925	marked "TW", character, glass eyes, open mouth
210	J.D. Kestner jr.	ca 1912	character, shoulder head, solid dome, sleep eyes, open /closed mouth
211	J.D. Kestner jr.	ca 1912	"JDK", character, sleep eyes, open or open /closed mouth
211	Fritz Dressel	GM 1926	"Dreso-doll"
211	Gebr. Knoch	ca 1912	"Made in Germany DRGM ", character, solid dome, painted eyes, closed smiling mouth, boy
212	Baehr & Proeschild	ca 1888	dolly face, glass eyes, closed mouth
212	Fritz Dressel	GM 1926	"Dreso-doll"
212	J.D. Kestner jr.	ca 1910	"JDK", character, painted or glass eyes, closed mouth
213	Baehr & Proeschild	ca 1888	dolly face
213	Hertwig & Co.	GM 1910	presumably character
214	Hertwig & Co.	GM 1910	presumably character

Mold No.	Firm	Date	Description and Identification
214	Kämmer & Reinhardt	GM 1909	character, shoulder head, painted eyes, closed mouth (Hans and Gretchen)(see mold # 114)
214	C.F. Kling	ca 1890	shoulder head, molded hair, glass eyes, closed mouth
214	J.D. Kestner jr.	ca 1910	"JDK", head with and without fur brows
215	J.D. Kestner jr.	ca 1910	"JDK", head with fur brows, sleep eyes, open mouth
215	Catterfelder	ca 1912	character, painted eyes, smiling, closed mouth
216	Gebr. Knoch	ca 1912	"GKN Ges.No.Gesch.", character, shoulder head, solid dome, painted eyes, laughing , open /closed mouth
216	J.D. Kestner jr.	ca 1912	dolly face
217	F&W. Goebel	ca 1900	"WG", dolly face, for Max Handwerck
217	Gebr. Knoch	ca 1912	"GKN", character, solid dome, laughing
217	C.F. Kling	ca 1885	shoulder head, molded hair, glass eyes, closed mouth
218	Catterfelder Puppenfabrik	ca 1912	character, solid dome, sleep eyes, open mouth with movable tongue
218	J.D. Kestner jr.	ca 1912	"JDK", character, solid dome, sleep eyes, open mouth
219	Baehr & Proeschild	ca 1888	dolly face, sleep eyes, open mouth

Mold No.	Firm	Date	Description and Identification
219	Catterfelder Puppenfabrik	ca 1912	"CP", character, painted eyes, closed mouth
219	Ernst Heubach	ca 1912	character, googly eyes, closed smiling mouth
219	J.D. Kestner jr.	GM 1912	presumably character
220	Baehr & Proeschild	ca 1888	dolly face, glass eyes, closed mouth, Oriental
220	Catterfelder Puppenfabrik	ca 1912	"CP", character, sleep eyes, open /closed smiling mouth
220	C.F. Kling	ca 1890	with bell, shoulder head, china or bisque, molded hair, painted face
220	Fritz Dressel	GM 1926	"Dreso-doll"
220	J.D. Kestner jr.	ca 1912	"JDK", character, sleep eyes, open /closed mouth
221	J.D. Kestner jr.	ca 1913	"JDK ges.gesch.", character, googly eyes, smiling, closed mouth (presumably made after Kewpie-Copyright by Rose O`Neill 1913)
221	Koenig & Wernicke	ca 1935	"K&W HARTGUMMI", character, sleep eyes, open mouth
221	Unknown	ca 1915	character, solid dome, sleep eyes, open /closed mouth with painted tongue
221	Gebr. Knoch	ca 1912	character, solid dome, painted eyes, open /closed mouth
223	Armand Marseille	ca 1913	"AM", character, googly eyes, closed mouth

Mold No.	Firm	Date	Description and Identification
223	Gebr. Knoch	ca 1912	"GKN GES.No.GESCH", character, shoulder head, solid dome, painted eyes, molded tears, closed mouth
223	C.F. Kling	ca 1890	shoulder head with molded hair, china with painted features
223	Hermann Steiner	GM 1926	"HS DRGM 954, 642", character with "living Steiner-eye"
223	Schützmeister & Quendt	ca 1925	"SQ", character, sleep eyes, open mouth
224	Baehr & Proeschild	GM 1888	head, glass eyes, closed or open mouth, also as Indian
224	Theodor Recknagel	ca 1925	character, molded cap
225	Baehr & Proeschild	GM 1888	dolly face
225	Armand Marseille	ca 1920	"AM", character, sleep eyes, open mouth
225	Fritz Dressel	GM 1926	"Dreso-doll"
225	Kämmer & Reinhardt	ca 1920	shoulder head, celluloid
225	C.F. Kling	ca 1890	shoulder head, molded hair, painted eyes, closed mouth
226	Baehr & Proeschild	GM 1888	dolly face
226	Theodor Recknagel	GM 1910	character
226	J.D. Kestner jr.	ca 1912	"JDK", character, sleep eyes, open mouth
227	Baehr & Proeschild	GM 1888	dolly face

Mold No.	Firm	Date	Description and Identification
227	Theodor Recknagel	GM 1910	character
229	Gebr. Knoch	ca 1912	character, solid dome, painted eyes, open /closed mouth
230	Baehr & Proeschild	ca 1888	dolly face, shoulder head, glass eyes, open or closed mouth, dolly face
230	Armand Marseille	ca 1912	"AM", with or without "Fany", character, solid dome, sleep eyes, closed mouth
230	Gebr. Knoch	ca 1912	"GKN", character, shoulder head, molded cap, painted eyes, open /closed laughing mouth
230	Fritz Dressel	GM 1926	"Dreso-doll"
231	Armand Marseille	GM 1912	"AM 248 Fany", character, sleep eyes, closed mouth
231	August Steiner Köppelsdorf	ca 1930	"A.S.", character, baby
232	Gebr. Knoch	ca 1912	"GKN", character, shoulder head, molded cap, painted eyes, open/closed laughing mouth
232	Theodor Recknagel	ca 1920	character, molded cap
232	Swaine & Co.	ca 1912	character, solid dome, glass eyes, open mouth, variation by "Lori" GM 1910 with closed mouth
233	Armand Marseille	ca 1920	with and without "AM", character, sleep eyes, open mouth

Mold No.	Firm	Date	Description and Identification
233	Gebr. Knoch	ca 1912	"MADE IN GERMANY Ges.No.Gesch.", character, shoulder head with molded cap, painted eye, open /closed laughing mouth
234	J.D. Kestner jr.	ca 1914	"JDK", character, shoulder head, solid dome, glass eyes, open or open /closed mouth
235	Ernst Heubach	ca 1905	dolly face
235	J.D. Kestner jr.	ca 1914	"JDK", character, shoulder head, glass eyes, open mouth
236	Ernst Heubach	ca 1905	dolly face
236	J.D. Kestner jr.	GM 1913	"JDK", character, sleep eyes, open mouth
237	Ernst Heubach	ca 1905	dolly face
237	J.D. Kestner jr.	GM 1914	with and without "JDK ges. gesch. 1070 Hilda" or "made in Germany 237 J.D.K.jr. 1914 C Hilda", character, sleep eyes, open mouth
237	Gebr. Knoch	ca 1912	"Made in Germany ges.gesch.", character, shoulder head with molded cap, painted eyes, laughing open /closed mouth with 2 teeth
238	Ernst Heubach	ca 1905	dolly face
238	Unknown	ca 1914	character, solid dome, painted eyes, closed mouth
238	Gebr. Knoch	ca 1912	character with molded hat, painted eyes, open /closed mouth, boy

Mold No.	Firm	Date	Description and Identification
239	Baehr & Proeschild	ca 1888	dolly face, glass eyes, closed mouth
239	J.D. Kestner jr.	ca 1914	"JDK", character, sleep eyes, open mouth
240	Armand Marseille	ca 1914	"AM", character, solid dome, painted googly eyes, closed mouth
240	Hermann Steiner	ca 1925	"HS", newborn, sleep eyes, closed mouth
240	Fritz Dressel	GM 1926	"Dreso-doll"
240	Unknown	ca 1914	Kewpie type, with molded hair-piece, solid dome, googly eyes, closed mouth
240	baby Phyllis Doll Co.	ca 1925	" baby PHYLLIS Made in Germany", newborn, flange neck, sleep eyes, closed mouth
241	Ernst Heubach	ca 1905	dolly face
241	Walther & Sohn	ca 1920	"W&S", shoulder head
241	Theodor Recknagel	ca 1925	"LA&S/R&A", newborn, sleep eyes, closed mouth, flange neck, for Louis Amberg & Son.
241	Unknown	ca 1925	"KB", newborn, flange neck, glass eyes, closed mouth or head, glass eyes, open mouth with 2 teeth
241	Unknown	ca 1914	Kewpie type, googly eyes, closed mouth
241	J.D. Kestner jr.	ca 1914	"JDK", character, sleep eyes, open mouth

Mold No.	Firm	Date	Description and Identification
241	Gebr. Knoch	ca 1912	character, shoulder head, molded hair, painted eyes, laughing mouth with painted teeth
242	Armand Marseille	ca 1930	"AM", character, painted bisque
242	Ernst Heubach	ca 1930	character, painted bisque
242	Hermann Steiner	ca 1926	"HS DRGM 954, 642", character with "living Steiner-eye"
242	Koenig & Wernicke	ca 19125	"K&W", character
242	Unknown	ca 1925	"KB", newborn, flange neck, glass eyes, closed mouth
242	J.D. Kestner jr.	ca 1914	"JDK", character, sleep eyes, open mouth
243	Hermann Steiner	ca 1926	"DRGM 954 642", character, molded hair, big glass eyes with glasses, laughing open /closed mouth ("living Steiner-eye")
243	J.D. Kestner jr.	ca 1914	"JDK", character, sleep eyes, open mouth, Oriental, also with all-bisque-body also with solid dome and painted, black hair
243	Unknown	ca 1920	character, solid dome, painted eyes, laughing open /closed mouth, 2 teeth below
244	Baehr & Proeschild	ca 1888	glass eyes, closed mouth, Indian
244	Armand Marseille	ca 1930	"AM", character, painted bisque
245	Hermann Steiner	ca 1925	"HS", character, glass eyes, closed mouth, baby

Mold No.	Firm	Date	Description and Identification
245	Baehr & Proeschild	ca 1888	dolly face, shoulder head, glass eyes, open mouth
245	Kämmer & Reinhardt	ca 1920	shoulder head, celluloid
245	J.D. Kestner jr.	GM 1914	"JDK jr. Hilda", character, sleep eyes, open mouth, also as Black doll
246	Armand Marseille	ca 1930	character, painted bisque
246	Baehr & Proeschild	ca 1888	dolly face, shoulder head
246	Hermann Steiner	ca 1920	"HS", character, baby, laughing
246	Gebr. Knoch	ca 1912	"GESCH", character with molded cap, painted googly eyes, grinning mouth, boy
246	Kämmer & Reinhardt	ca 1920	shoulder head, celluloid or "S&H K&R" in bisque
246	J.D. Kestner jr.	GM 1915	"JDK", character, sleep eyes, open mouth
247	Baehr & Proeschild	GM 1889	"DEP", dolly face, sleep eyes, open mouth, also as Black doll
247	C.F. Kling	ca 1890	shoulder head, glass eyes, closed mouth
247	Hermann Steiner	ca 1926	"HS DRGM 954642", character with "living Steiner-eye"
247	Unknown	ca 1925	"KB", newborn, flange neck, glass eyes, closed mouth
247	J.D. Kestner jr.	GM 1915	"JDK", character, sleep eyes, open mouth
248	Baehr & Proeschild	GM 1889	dolly face

Mold No.	Firm	Date	Description and Identification
248	Kämmer & Reinhardt	ca 1920	shoulder head, celluloid or bisque
249	J.D. Kestner jr.	ca 1915	"JDK", character, sleep eyes, open mouth
250	Baehr & Proeschild	ca 1890	dolly face
250	J.D. Kestner jr.	ca 1920	"JDK", Walküre, dolly face, for Kley & Hahn
250	Armand Marseille	GM 1912	"AM DRGM 248 GB", character, solid dome, painted eyes, open mouth, for Geo. Borgfeldt & Co.
250	Ernst Heubach	ca 1914	"Heubach, Köppelsdorf", character, with or without pierced nostrils, sleep eyes, open mouth
250	Walther & Sohn	ca 1920	"W&S", character, shoulder head
251	Baehr & Proeschild	GM 1889	dolly face
251	Armand Marseille	GM 1912	"AM 248", character, baby, sleep eyes, open /closed mouth with molded tongue, for Geo. Borgfeldt & Co.
251	Ernst Heubach	ca 1914	"Heubach, Köppelsdorf", character, sleep eyes, open mouth
252	Baehr & Proeschild	GM 1889	"DEP", dolly face, glass eyes, open mouth
252	Schützmeister & Quendt	ca 1920	"SQ", character, Black doll
252	Ernst Heubach	ca 1914	character, solid dome, sleep eyes, closed mouth, Black doll with molded hair, painted eyes, closed mouth

Mold No.	Firm	Date	Description and Identification
252	Armand Marseille	GM 1912	"AM 248", character, solid dome with molded hair, painted eyes, closed smiling mouth (Kewpie-type)
253	Baehr & Proeschild	GM 1889	dolly face
253	Armand Marseille	ca 1925	"AM Nobbikid Reg.U.S.Pat.O66 Germany", character, googly eyes, closed mouth
254	Armand Marseille	ca 1912	"AM", character, solid dome, painted eyes, closed mouth
254	C.F. Kling	ca 1890	with bell, shoulder head, molded hair, painted eyes, closed mouth
254	J.D. Kestner jr.	GM 1916	presumably character
255	Armand Marseille	ca 1920	character, solid dome, painted eyes, closed mouth
255	Kämmer & Reinhardt	ca 1920	shoulder head, celluloid
255	Porzellanfabrik Mengersgereuth	ca 1920	"PM", character, googly eyes, closed mouth
255	J.D. Kestner jr.	ca 1916	"O.I.C. made in Germany", character, solid dome, tiny glass eyes, open /closed crying mouth
256	Armand Marseille	ca 1920	"AM" with and without "Maar", character, baby, for E.Maar & Sohn
256	Kämmer & Reinhardt	ca 1920	shoulder head, celluloid
257	J.D. Kestner jr.	ca 1916	"JDK", character, sleep eyes, open mouth

Mold No.	Firm	Date	Description and Identification
258	Armand Marseille	ca 1913	"AM", character, googly eyes, closed mouth
259	Baehr & Proeschild	GM 1890	dolly face
259	Armand Marseille	ca 1920	"AM GB", character, baby, for Geo. Borgfeldt & Co.
259	Ernst Heubach	ca 1914	character
260	Baehr & Proeschild	GM 1890	"dep", dolly face, glass eyes, closed mouth
260	Ernst Heubach	GM 1914	character, shoulder head, molded hair, painted eyes, open /closed mouth with molded tongue and teeth
260	J.D. Kestner jr.	ca 1916	"JDK", character, sleep eyes, open mouth
261	Baehr & Proeschild	GM 1890	"DEP", dolly face, glass eyes, closed mouth
261	Ernst Heubach	GM 1914	character
261	August Steiner, Köppelsdorf	ca 1930	"AS", character, composition, also as black doll
262	Baehr & Proeschild	GM 1890	dolly face
262	Catterfelder Puppenfabrik	ca 1916	character, sleep eyes, open mouth, movable tongue
262	Ernst Heubach	GM 1914	"EH DRGM ", character, solid dome with molded hair, painted googly eyes, closed mouth
262	J.D. Kestner jr.	ca 1916	"K&Co", character, sleep eyes, open mouth

Mold No.	Firm	Date	Description and Identification
263	C.F. Kling	ca 1900	"bell", dolly face
263	Catterfelder Puppenfabrik	ca 1916	"CP", character, sleep eyes, open mouth
263	Baehr & Proeschild	GM 1890	dolly face
263	Ernst Heubach	GM 1914	character
263	J.D. Kestner jr.	ca 1916	"JDK" or "K&Co", character, sleep eyes, open mouth, with "CP" also for Catterfelder Puppenfabrik
264	Baehr & Proeschild	GM 1890	dolly face
264	Ernst Heubach	GM 1914	character
264	J.D. Kestner jr.	ca 1916	"K&CO", character, sleep eyes, open mouth, with "CP" also for Catterfelder Puppenfabrik
265	Baehr & Proeschild	GM 1890	dolly face
265	Rempel & Breitung	ca 1925	"RB/117", dolly face, glass eyes, open mouth
265	Kämmer & Reinhardt	ca 1908	shoulder head, celluloid
266	Armand Marseille	ca 1930	"AM", head, molded braids, glass eyes, open mouth
266	Ernst Heubach	GM 1915	character, solid dome, painted eyes, smiling, closed mouth
266	C.F. Kling	ca 1900	"bell", shoulder head with molded hair, glass eyes, open /closed mouth with molded teeth
266	Kestner & Comp.	ca 1920	character for Kley & Hahn, see mold 680

Mold No.	Firm	Date	Description and Identification
267	Ernst Heubach	GM 1914	"DRGM ", character, glass eyes, open mouth with 2 teeth below
268	Ernst Heubach	GM 1914	character
269	Baehr & Proeschild	ca 1890	"DEP", dolly face
269	Ernst Heubach	GM 1914	"EH", character, solid dome, painted eyes, closed mouth
269	Franz Schmidt & Co.	ca 1900	"S&C", dolly face
270	Baehr & Proeschild	ca 1890	"DEP", dolly face, shoulder head, glass eyes, closed mouth
270	Armand Marseille	ca 1920	"AM", shoulder head
270	Catterfelder Puppenfabrik	ca 1920	character
271	Ernst Heubach	GM 1914	"EH", shoulder head, solid dome, painted eyes, closed mouth
271	Unknown	ca 1915	character, painted googly eyes, smiling, closed mouth
272	J.D. Kestner jr.	ca 1925	"Siegfried made in Germany", newborn, flange neck, sleep eyes, closed mouth
273	Baehr & Proeschild	GM 1891	"DEP", dolly face, sleep eyes, closed or open mouth
273	Armand Marseille	ca 1939	"AM", shoulder head, composition
275	Baehr & Proeschild	GM 1891	dolly face, glass eyes, open mouth
275	Ernst Heubach	ca 1915	shoulder head, dolly face

Mold No.	Firm	Date	Description and Identification
275	Armand Marseille	ca 1936	"AM", shoulder head, made in painted bisque or composition
276	Armand Marseille	ca 1936	"AM", shoulder head, made in painted bisque or composition
276	Ernst Heubach	GM 1915	"EH", character, solid dome, painted eyes, closed mouth with molded bee on top of the nose
277	Baehr & Proeschild	GM 1891	„DEP". doll y face, also as black doll
278	Baehr & Proeschild	GM 1891	"dep", dolly face, shoulder head, sleep eyes, open mouth
279	J.D. Kestner jr.	ca 1925	"Germany CENTURY DOLL & Co", newborn
281	Baehr & Proeschild	GM 1892	dolly face
281	Ernst Heubach	GM 1915	character
281	J.D. Kestner jr.	ca 1925	"CENTURY DOLL & Co Kestner Germany", newborn, flange neck, sleep eyes, open /closed mouth
282	Ernst Heubach	GM 1915	character
282	J.D. Kestner jr.	ca 1920	"Walküre", dolly face, for Kley & Hahn
283	Baehr & Proeschild	GM 1892	dolly face
283	Ernst Heubach	GM 1915	"EH", shoulder head, character, molded hair and 2 bows, painted eyes, open /closed mouth
283	F&W. Goebel	ca 1900	dolly face, for Max Handwerck
284	Ernst Heubach	GM 1915	character

Mold No.	Firm	Date	Description and Identification
285	Baehr & Proeschild	GM 1892	dolly face
285	F&W. Goebel	ca 1900	dolly face, for Max Handwerck
285	C.F. Kling	ca 1890	shoulder head, molded hair, china, painted features
286	F&W. Goebel	ca 1900	"Bebe Elite", dolly face, for Max Handwerck
287	Baehr & Proeschild	GM 1892	dolly face
288	Armand Marseille	ca 1910	"Queen Louise Germany", dolly face
289	Baehr & Proeschild	GM 1892	"DEP", dolly face
289	Ernst Heubach	ca 1915	"EH", character, molded hair, painted googly eyes, closed mouth with molded, stuck out tongue
290	C.F. Kling	ca 1890	with bell, shoulder head, molded hair, painted eyes, closed mouth
290	Simon & Halbig	ca 1910	"K&R Halbig", character, sleep eyes, open mouth, for Kämmer & Reinhardt
291	Baehr & Proeschild	ca 1892	"dep", dolly face
291	Ernst Heubach	ca 1915	"EH", character, glass eyes, closed mouth
292	Unknown	ca 1913	character, googly eyes, closed smiling mouth
292	Baehr & Proeschild	GM 1892	dolly face
292	Ernst Heubach	ca 1915	"EH", character, solid dome, sleep eyes, open mouth

Mold No.	Firm	Date	Description and Identification
292	J.D. Kestner jr.	ca 1930	"KH 1930", character, for Kley & Hahn
293	Franz Schmidt & Co.	ca 1900	"S&C", dolly face
293	Carl Knoll, Böhmen	ca 1900	"CK", dolly face, shoulder head, glass eyes, open mouth
297	Baehr & Proeschild	GM 1893	dolly face
298	Koenig & Wernicke	ca 1930	"KW" with turtle-mark, celluloid, character, glass eyes, open mouth
300	Unknown	ca 1890	"TR", dolly face, glass eyes, closed mouth
300	Ernst Heubach	ca 1920	"Heubach, Köppelsdorf", character, sleep eyes, open mouth
300	Armand Marseille	ca 1925	"AM/MH", flapper, glass eyes, closed mouth
300	C.F. Kling	ca 1890	with bell, shoulder head, molded hair, painted eyes, closed mouth
300	Schützmeister & Quendt	ca 1920	"SQ", character, baby
300	Oskar Bauer	GM 1926	baby
300	Baehr & Proeschild	ca 1893	dolly face, swivel head
301	Kämmer & Reinhardt	ca 1910	shoulder head, character, celluloid, painted eyes, closed mouth, see also mold number 101
301	Baehr & Proeschild	GM 1893	dolly face
301	Ernst Heubach	ca 1920	head

Mold No.	Firm	Date	Description and Identification
301	Wiefel & Co.	ca 1912	"W&Co", dolly face
301	Schützmeister & Quendt	ca 1920	"SQ", character, baby (found also with date "18.1.21")
302	Baehr & Proeschild	GM 1893	dolly face, glass eyes, closed mouth
302	Ernst Heubach	ca 1920	character, sleep eyes, open mouth
302	Unknown	ca 1910	clown, solid dome, painted, laughing face
303	C.F. Kling	GM 1897	soldier head with molded cap, painted eyes, closed mouth, molded moustache
304	Nicole B. Döbrich	GM 1892	dolly face
305	Louis Wolf & Co.	ca 1910	"Germany Queen Louise", dolly face, sleep eyes, open mouth, presumably from Armand Marseille
305	Baehr & Proeschild	GM 1893	dolly face
305	C.F. Kling	GM 1897	soldier head with molded cap, painted eyes, closed mouth, molded moustache
305	Nicole B. Döbrich	GM 1892	dolly face
306	Baehr & Proeschild	GM 1893	"dep", dolly face
309	Baehr & Proeschild	ca 1893	dolly face, shoulder head, glass eyes, open mouth
309	Armand Marseille	ca 1920	shoulder head, glass eyes, open mouth

Mold No.	Firm	Date	Description and Identification
310	Armand Marseille	ca 1929	"AM JUST ME", character, googly eyes, little closed mouth, for Geo. Borgfeldt & Co.
312	Ernst Heubach	ca 1922	"SUR" or "Heubach, Köppelsdorf", character, for Seyfarth & Reinhardt
313	Baehr & Proeschild	GM 1893	dolly face
313	Ernst Heubach	ca 1922	"SUR", character, for Seyfarth & Reinhardt
317	F&W. Goebel	GM 1913	presumably character
317	Ernst Heubach	ca 1920	character
318	Armand Marseille	ca 1930	"AM", character, solid dome, sleep eyes, open mouth, black doll
318	Ernst Heubach	GM 1923	"EH", character, googly eyes, closed mouth or marked with "AH Schalkau Heubach Köppelsdorf" for Albin Hess (GM-owner)
319	Ernst Heubach	GM 1923	"EH", character, googly eyes, whining, or marked with "AH Schalkau Heubach Köppelsdorf" for Albin Hess (GM-owner)
319	F&W. Goebel	GM 1913	presumably character
320	Baehr & Proeschild	GM 1894	"B&P dep", dolly face
320	Armand Marseille	GM 1913	"AM 255", character, solid dome, painted googly eyes, closed mouth
320	Ernst Heubach	ca 1920	character, with pierced nostrils, sleep eyes, open mouth
320	F&W. Goebel	GM 1913	presumably character

Mold No.	Firm	Date	Description and Identification
321	Baehr & Proeschild	GM 1894	dolly face
321	Ernst Heubach	ca 1920	character with pierced nostrils, sleep eyes, open mouth
321	F&W. Goebel	GM 1913	presumably character
321	Unknown	ca 1914	"Ges.gesch.", character, googly eyes
321	Kämmer & Reinhardt	ca 1930	flange neck, celluloid
322	Baehr & Proeschild	GM 1894	dolly face
322	Armand Marseille	ca 1914	"AM", character, solid dome with molded hair, painted googly eyes, closed smiling mouth
322	Ernst Heubach	ca 1915	character, googly eyes, closed, smiling mouth
322	F&W. Goebel	GM 1913	presumably character
323	Baehr & Proeschild	GM 1894	dolly face
323	Armand Marseille	ca 1914	"AM", character, googly eyes, closed mouth, also in composition
324	Baehr & Proeschild	GM 1894	dolly face
324	Armand Marseille	GM 1913	"AM 255", character, solid dome, painted googly eyes, closed mouth
325	Baehr & Proeschild	ca 1894	dolly face, sleep eyes, open mouth with molded teeth
325	Armand Marseille	ca 1915	character, googly eyes, closed mouth

Mold No.	Firm	Date	Description and Identification
326	Armand Marseille	GM 1913	"AM 259", character, solid dome, glass eyes, open mouth
327	Armand Marseille	GM 1913	"AM 259", character, baby, for Geo. Borgfeldt & Co
328	Armand Marseille	GM 1913	"AM 267", character, baby, for Geo. Borgfeldt & Co.
329	Armand Marseille	GM 1913	"AM 267", character, baby, for Geo. Borgfeldt & Co.
330	Baehr & Proeschild	ca 1894	dolly face
330	F&W. Goebel	ca 1900	dolly face
333	Armand Marseille	ca 1925	"AM", character, solid dome, black doll or Oriental
333	Koenig & Wernicke	ca 1935	"NICAPUT", character
334	Ernst Heubach	ca 1924	character, glass eyes, open mouth, black doll
338	Ernst Heubach	ca 1925	newborn, character, solid dome, sleep eyes, closed mouth
339	Ernst Heubach	ca 1925	newborn, character, solid dome, sleep eyes, closed mouth, also as black doll or Oriental
340	Baehr & Proeschild	ca 1894	"DEP", dolly face, glass eyes, open mouth
340	F&W. Goebel	ca 1900	dolly face
340	Ernst Heubach	ca 1925	newborn, solid dome, sleep eyes, closed mouth

Mold No.	Firm	Date	Description and Identification
340	Armand Marseille	ca 1925	newborn, solid dome, sleep eyes, closed mouth
341	Vereinigte Köppelsdorfer Porzellanfabr.	GM 1926	"AM", newborn, flange neck, solid dome, sleep eyes, closed mouth, also as black doll and Mulatto, My Dream baby
341k	Vereinigte Köppelsdorfer Porzellanfabr.	GM 1926	"AM", newborn, head, solid dome, sleep eyes, closed mouth, My Dream baby, also as Oriental
341 Ka	Vereinigte Köppelsdorfer Porzellanfabr.	GM 1926	"AM", newborn, with wig, sleep eyes, closed mouth
342	Baehr & Proeschild	GM 1895	dolly face
342	Vereinigte Köppelsdorfer Porzellanfabr.	GM 1926	doll head
342	Ernst Heubach	ca 1926	"Heubach Köppelsdorf", character, sleep eyes, open mouth, also as black doll, often with pacifer-pull-voice, also in composition with painted eyes
342	Armand Marseille	ca 1926	"AM", newborn, solid dome, sleep eyes, open /closed mouth
343	Baehr & Proeschild	GM 1895	dolly face
343	Vereinigte Köppelsdorfer Porzellanfabr.	GM 1927	baby
344	Ernst Heubach	ca 1926	character, sleep eyes, open mouth, black doll
345	Vereinigte Köppelsdorfer Porzellanfabr.	GM 1926	baby

Mold No.	Firm	Date	Description and Identification
345	Armand Marseille	ca 1926	"AM Germany Kiddiejoy", character
347	Armand Marseille	ca 1926	character, shoulder head, sleep eyes, closed crying mouth
348	Baehr & Proeschild	GM 1895	dolly face
348	Ernst Heubach	ca 1926	newborn, solid dome, glass eyes, closed mouth
349	Ernst Heubach	ca 1926	newborn, solid dome, sleep eyes, closed mouth
350	Baehr & Proeschild	GM 1895	"dep", shoulder head, dolly face
350	F&W. Goebel	GM 1893	shoulder head, glass eyes, open mouth, dolly face
350	Vereinigte Köppelsdorfer Porzellanfabr.	GM 1926	baby
350	Ernst Heubach	ca 1926	"Heubach Köppelsdorf", character, sleep eyes, open mouth
350	Armand Marseille	ca 1926	"AM", character, sleep eyes, closed mouth
351	Vereinigte Köppelsdorfer Porzellanfabr.	GM 1926	baby
351	Armand Marseille	ca 1926	"AM", newborn, flange neck, sleep eyes, open mouth, My Dream baby, also as black doll
351k	Armand Marseille	ca 1926	"AM", newborn, head, sleep eyes, open mouth, also as black doll, My Dream baby

Mold No.	Firm	Date	Description and Identification
351	Kämmer & Reinhardt	ca 1935	"K&RW", character, celluloid, flirting eyes, open mouth
352	Vereinigte Köppelsdorfer Porzellanfabr.	GM 1930	"AM", newborn, solid dome, sleep eyes, open mouth
353	Armand Marseille	ca 1926	"AM", newborn, solid dome, sleep eyes, closed mouth, also as black doll or Oriental
353	Ernst Heubach (presumably)	GM 1930	"Priska Sander Neustadt/Orla 353 DRGM 2", two-face-doll, newborn, laughing: sleep eyes, open mouth, crying: little sleep eyes with molded tears, open mouth
354	Unknown	ca 1900	lady with molded hair, painted features
355	Baehr & Proeschild	ca 1896	dolly face, glass eyes, open mouth
355k	Armand Marseille	ca 1926	newborn, sleep eyes, closed mouth
356	Armand Marseille	ca 1926	"AM", newborn, sleep eyes, closed mouth, Oriental
359	Adolf Wislizenus	ca 1923	character
360a	Armand Marseille	GM 1913	"AM 252", character, sleep eyes, open mouth
362k	Armand Marseille	ca 1926	character, molded hair, painted or sleep eyes, open mouth, black doll
363	Armand Marseille	ca 1930	"AM", black doll, in composition
365	Sonneberger Porzellanfabriken	ca 1948	"SP", black doll

Mold No.	Firm	Date	Description and Identification
369	Armand Marseille	ca 1938	closed mouth, composition
370	C.F. Kling	ca 1900	dolly face, sleep eyes, open mouth
370	Armand Marseille	ca 1900	"AM", shoulder head, dolly face (1938 also in bisque and composition)
370	Max F. Schelhorn	ca 1912	"SS" incised in shield, character, two-face-doll, laughing and crying
371	Armand Marseille	ca 1926	"AM L.A.& S.DRGM ", character, newborn, solid dome, glass eyes, open mouth, drink baby, for Louis Amberg & Son
372	C.F. Kling	ca 1900	dolly face
372	Armand Marseille	ca 1925	"AM Germany Kiddijoy", character, shoulder head, molded hair, painted eyes, open /closed mouth laughing with 2 uper teeth
373	C.F. Kling	ca 1900	dolly face, shoulder head
374	Baehr & Proeschild	GM 1896	dolly face
375	Baehr & Proeschild	GM 1896	dolly face
375	Armand Marseille	ca 1925	"AM Germany Kiddijoy", character, shoulder head, molded hair, painted eyes, open /closed mouth, laughing, 2 upper teeth
376	Baehr & Proeschild	GM 1896	dolly face
376	Armand Marseille	ca 1905	"AM", shoulder head, dolly face

Mold No.	Firm	Date	Description and Identification
377	C.F. Kling	ca 1900	with bell or with bell and star, for Kämmer & Reinhardt, shoulder head, dolly face, glass eyes, open mouth
377	Armand Marseille	ca 1938	"AM", head, boy and girl, composition
378	Baehr & Proeschild	GM 1896	dolly face
378	Armand Marseille	ca 1930	"AM", head, composition
379	Baehr & Proeschild	GM 1896	"B&P dep", dolly face, head, glass eyes, open mouth
380	Baehr & Proeschild	GM 1896	dolly face
381	Baehr & Proeschild	GM 1896	dolly face
382	Armand Marseille	ca 1930	"AM", newborn, solid dome, sleep eyes, open mouth
383	Hertwig & Co.	GM 1910	presumably character
384	Armand Marseille	ca 1905	"AM", head, dolly face
384	Hertwig & Co.	GM 1910	presumably character
385	Hertwig & Co.	GM 1910	presumably character
385	Armand Marseille	ca 1930	"AM", character, painted eyes with inserted eye-lashes, closed mouth, composition
385	Unknown	ca 1925	character, newborn, solid dome, painted eyes, closed mouth
386	Hertwig & Co.	GM 1910	presumably character

Mold No.	Firm	Date	Description and Identification
388	Unknown	ca 1900	"dep", molded blonde hair, glass eyes, closed mouth
389	Baehr & Proeschild	GM 1897	dolly face
390	Ernst Heubach	ca 1927	character, solid dome, sleep eyes, open mouth
390	Baehr & Proeschild	GM 1897	dolly face
390	Armand Marseille	ca 1900	"AM", head, dolly face
390	Armand Marseille	ca 1909	"AM DRGM 377439 DRGM 374830 DRGM 374831", head, with fur brows
390	Unknown	ca 1925	"SWC", character, solid dome, painted eyes, open /closed mouth (mold number also found on all bisque body)
390n	Armand Marseille	GM 1912	"AM 246", head, dolly face
391	Armand Marseille	GM 1936	"AM", head, dolly face
391	Unknown	ca 1925	"SWC", character, glass eyes, open/closed mouth, tongue (mold number also found on all bisque body)
391	Hermann Steiner	ca 1930	"HS", Boudoir-Doll
393	Vereinigte Köppelsdorfer Porzellanfabr.	GM 1927	baby
393	Unknown	ca 1925	character, googly eyes, closed mouth
393	Baehr & Proeschild	GM 1897	dolly face

Mold No.	Firm	Date	Description and Identification
394	Baehr & Proeschild	ca 1897	"B&P" or only with mold number, head, dolly face, glass eyes, open mouth
395	Armand Marseille	ca 1925	"AM", character, sleep eyes, open mouth
396	Vereinigte Köppelsdorfer Porzellanfabr.	GM 1930	character, black doll
396	Ernst Heubach	GM 1930	"EH", newborn, flange neck, glass eyes, closed mouth, black doll
396	Armand Marseille	ca 1936	"AM", Oriental
398	Armand Marseille	ca 1927	"AM", newborn, solid dome, glass eyes, closed mouth, Oriental
399	Vereinigte Köppelsdorfer Porzellanfabr.	GM 1930	character, black doll
399	Ernst Heubach	GM 1930	"Heubach, Köppelsdorf", with or without "DRGM ", solid dome, sleep eyes, closed mouth, white or black doll, South-Sea- baby, also for Luge & Co.
399	Armand Marseille	GM 1936	"AM", character
400	Vereinigte Köppelsdorfer Porzellanfabr.	GM 1926	"AM 343", character, sleep eyes, closed mouth, on flapper-body, see also mold number 401
400	Ernst Heubach	ca 1925	newborn, character, baby, painted hair, sleep eyes, open mouth
400	Oskar Bauer	GM 1926	head, celluloid, soft stuffed, leather body

Mold No.	Firm	Date	Description and Identification
400	Unknown	ca 1925	"SWC", character, sleep eyes, open mouth
400	Unknown	ca 1910	dolly face, sleep eyes, open or open/closed mouth
401	Armand Marseille	ca 1926	"AM", character, sleep eyes, open mouth, on flapper-body, see mold number 400
401	Simon & Halbig	ca 1910	"S&H K&R", glass eyes, open mouth, for Kämmer & Reinhardt
401	Hermann Steiner	ca 1912	"HS", character, shoulder head, solid dome, painted eyes, open/closed mouth, laughing
401	Berthold Kühn	GM 1928	newspaper-boy
401	Unknown	ca 1920	character, googly eyes, closed mouth
402	Simon & Halbig	ca 1910	"S&H K&R", head, glass eyes, open mouth, for Kämmer & Reinhardt
402	Armand Marseille	ca 1926	"AM", character, glass eyes, open mouth, on flapper-body
402	Berthold Kühn	GM 1928	golf-boy
402	Hermann Steiner	ca 1912	"HS", character, shoulder head, glass eyes, open/closed laughing mouth (wiged version of mold # 401)
403	Simon & Halbig	ca 1910	"S&H K&R", head, glass eyes, open mouth, for Kämmer & Reinhardt, also as Mulatto

Mold No.	Firm	Date	Description and Identification
405	Unknown	ca 1920	character, painted eyes, closed mouth
406	Kämmer & Reinhardt	ca 1908	"K&R", with turtle-mark, head, celluloid, glass eyes, open mouth
406	Armand Marseille	ca 1920	"AM", black doll
406	Ernst Heubach	ca 1920	"Heubach Köppelsdorf", glass eyes, open mouth, 2 teeth below, black doll
407	Carl Bergner	GM 1879	doll dressed in nighty
407	Ernst Heubach	ca 1920	"EH", character, sleep eyes, open mouth
408	J.D. Kestner jr. (presumably)	ca 1927	"Germany", shoulder head, glass eyes, closed mouth
409	Ernst Heubach	ca 1920	dolly face
409	J.D. Kestner jr. (presumably)	ca 1927	"Germany", shoulder head, glass eyes, closed mouth
410	Armand Marseille	GM 1913	"Germany", character, sleep eyes, open mouth, with movable jaw, for Robert Maaser or "AM DRGM ", but without movable jaw
410	Koenig & Wernicke	ca 1925	"K&W", character, flange neck, baby
410	Baehr & Proeschild	ca 1900	shoulder head, glass eyes, open mouth
410	Franz Schmidt & Co.	ca 1930	character, sleep eyes, open mouth, composition
410	Unknown	ca 1925	"Germany", solid dome, newborn, glass eyes, closed mouth, black doll

Mold No.	Firm	Date	Description and Identification
411	Armand Marseille	ca 1930	"AM", character, baby, composition
414	Ernst Heubach	ca 1925	newborn, solid dome, sleep eyes, open mouth, black doll
414	Armand Marseille	ca 1937	"AM", glass eyes, closed mouth, composition
415	Ernst Heubach	ca 1925	"Heubach Köppelsdorf", character with molded hair, sleep eyes, open laughing mouth
418	Ernst Heubach	ca 1926	character, solid dome, molded hair, glass eyes, open , laughing mouth, black doll, ("Pirat-Baby")
420	Heinrich Handwerck	ca 1921	"HH Germany", character
421	Heinrich Handwerck	ca 1921	"Germany Handwerck", character, sleep eyes, open mouth
421	Albin Peterhänsel	GM 1926	cobbler boy
422	Unknown	ca 1900	dolly face, sleep eyes, open mouth
425	Baehr & Proeschild	ca 1920	"Herz", character, solid dome, painted eyes, closed mouth
427	Ernst Heubach	ca 1926	character, sleep eyes open mouth
430	Armand Marseille	ca 1925	shoulder head, character, solid dome, painted eyes, closed mouth
435	Unknown	ca 1925	character, sleep eyes, open mouth
435	Franz Schmidt & Co.	ca 1938	"FS&Co", character, molded hair, composition

Mold No.	Firm	Date	Description and Identification
437	Ernst Heubach	ca 1926	character, solid dome, sleep eyes, closed mouth
437	Franz Schmidt & Co.	ca 1938	"FS&Co", character, flange neck, solid dome, flirting sleep eyes, open mouth
438	Franz Schmidt & Co.	ca 1928	"FS&Co.", character, flange neck, sleep eyes, open mouth
438	Ernst Heubach	ca 1926	character, sleep eyes, open mouth
439	Ernst Heubach	ca 1926	character, googly eyes, closed mouth
439	Franz Schmidt & Co.	ca 1938	"FS&Co", character, flange neck, sleep eyes, open mouth, composition
440	Unknown	ca 1905	dolly face, glass eyes, open mouth
444	Ernst Heubach	ca 1926	character, sleep eyes, closed mouth, black doll
444	Bähr & Proeschild	ca 1905	dolly face, glass eyes, open mouth
445	Ernst Heubach	ca 1925	character, two-face-doll, black face laughing, withe face crying
448	Bähr & Proeschild	ca 1905	dolly face, glass eyes, open mouth
448	Ernst Heubach	ca 1926	character, black doll or Indian
449	Unknown	ca 1905	dolly face, glass eyes, open mouth
449	Armand Marseille	ca 1930	"AM", head, painted eyes, closed mouth, composition or in bisque with glass eyes and closed mouth

Mold No.	Firm	Date	Description and Identification
450	Simon & Halbig	ca 1890	"Dep", multi-face-doll, laughing, crying, sleeping
450	Armand Marseille	ca 1938	"AM", head, sleep eyes, closed mouth, composition
450	Ernst Heubach	ca 1930	composition, glass eyes, closed mouth
451	Unknown	ca 1905	dolly face, glass eyes, open mouth
451	Ernst Heubach	ca 1928	character, solid dome, glass eyes, open mouth, black doll
451	Armand Marseille	ca 1936	"AM", head, sleep eyes, open mouth, Indian
452	Ernst Heubach	ca 1928	character, solid dome, glass eyes, open mouth, Gypsy or Oriental
453	Armand Marseille	ca 1936	"AM 453", head, rubber, glass eyes, open mouth, Shirley Temple
453	Franz Schmidt & Co.	ca 1935	"FS&Co.", Max and Moritz from composition with flirting eyes
453	Armand Marseille	ca 1936	"AM 452H", same as before, only with molded hair
454	Armand Marseille	ca 1930	head, composition
454	Franz Schmidt & Co.	ca 1938	"FS&Co", flange neck, solid dome with molded black hair
455	Unknown	ca 1925	character, googly eyes, closed smiling mouth
457	Unknown	ca 1905	dolly face

Mold No.	Firm	Date	Description and Identification
458	Ernst Heubach	ca 1930	character, black doll
458	Armand Marseille	ca 1936	character, Indian, in porcelain and composition
459	Ernst Heubach	ca 1930	character, solid dome, glass eyes, black doll, open mouth with big lower lip
463	Ernst Heubach	ca 1930	character, solid dome, sleep eyes, open mouth, black doll, laughing
471	Ernst Heubach	ca 1930	"Heubach Köppelsdorf", character, sleep eyes, closed mouth
476	Unknown	ca 1905	dolly face
478	Unknown	ca 1905	dolly face, sleep eyes, open mouth
489	Unknown	ca 1900	mask face from bisque, sleep eyes, open mouth (Carl-Bergner-doll)
480	Ernst Heubach	GM 1928	character, solid dome, South-Sea-Baby, for A. Luge & Co.
482	Unknown	ca 1926	newborn
498	Franz Schmidt & Co.	ca 1930	"FS&Co.", character, baby,metall
499	Unknown	ca 1900	dolly face, shoulder head
500	Simon & Halbig	GM 1910	presumably character
500	Bruno Schmidt	ca 1905	"BSW" with heart, glass eyes, open mouth, Oriental
500	Armand Marseille	GM 1910	"AM 232" or "DRGM ", character, solid dome, painted eyes, closed mouth

Mold No.	Firm	Date	Description and Identification
500	Armand Marseille	ca 1938	"AM", dolly face, glass eyes, closed mouth, composition (no likeness to bisque mold # 500)
500	Sonneberger Porzellanfabriken	ca 1948	"SP", dolly face, glass eyes, closed mouth (same model as Armand Marseille, ca 1938, mold number 500)
500	Hermann von Berg	GM 1926	"HvB", newborn, flange neck, sleep eyes, open mouth
500	Arthur Schoenau	ca 1926	"MB", newborn, flange neck, sleep eyes, open mouth (MB = My Cherub)
500k	Hermann von Berg	GM 1926	"HvB", newborn, head, sleep eyes, open mouth
501	F&W. Goebel	ca 1912	"WG" with crown, character, shoulder head, solid dome, painted eyes, open/closed laughing, mouth with molded teeth
501	Hermann von Berg	GM 1926	new born baby, open mouth
501	Guido Knauth	ca 1900	"Knauth", dolly face, glass eyes, open mouth, also as black doll
501	Franz Kiesewetter	GM 1912	whistler
502	Franz Kiesewetter	GM 1912	laughing girl
502	Catterfelder Puppenfabrik	ca 1910	dolly face, glass eyes, open mouth
503	Franz Kiesewetter	GM 1912	laughing boy

Mold No.	Firm	Date	Description and Identification
503	Unknown	ca 1880	"TR", dolly face, solid dome with 2 or 3 holes, glass eyes, closed mouth
503	Carl Kochniss	ca 1930	"Kochniss", sleep eyes, open mouth, black doll
504	Franz Kiesewetter	GM 1912	girl with googly eyes
504	Armand Marseille	ca 1930	"AM", head, composition
505	Franz Kiesewetter	GM 1913	boy with hat
505	Armand Marseille	ca 1938	"AM", sailer head, painted eyes, composition
506	Unknown	ca 1880	"TR", dolly face, solid dome with 2 or 3 holes, glass eyes, closed mouth
507	Franz Kiesewetter	GM 1913	boy without hat
509	Franz Kiesewetter	GM 1913	boy with painted eyes
510	Franz Kiesewetter	GM 1913	sly fellow with glass googly eyes
510	Armand Marseille	ca 1930	"AM", head, composition
510	Erste Steinbacher Porzellanfabrik	ca 1926	"GH", character, painted eyes, closed mouth
510	Unknown	ca 1880	"HL", dolly face, solid dome with 2 or 3 holes, glass eyes, closed mouth
511	Franz Kiesewetter	GM 1913	sly fellow with painted googly eyes
513	Armand Marseille	ca 1920	"AM", sleep eyes, open mouth, black doll

Mold No.	Firm	Date	Description and Identification
513	Franz Kiesewetter	GM 1913	crying boy
513	Unknown	ca 1905	dolly face, sleep eyes, open mouth
514	Franz Kiesewetter	GM 1913	crying girl
514	Heber & Co.	ca 1905	"HC", dolly face, glass eyes, open mouth
514	Armand Marseille	ca 1935	"Germany", flange neck, solid dome, glass eyes, open mouth, composition
515	Franz Kiesewetter	GM 1914	crying boy without cap
515	Armand Marseille	ca 1930	"AM", head, composition
516	Franz Kiesewetter	GM 1914	crying girl without cap
516	Armand Marseille	ca 1930	"AM", head, composition
517	Franz Kiesewetter	GM 1914	shock-headed Peter
518	Armand Marseille	ca 1938	"AM", socket or flange neck, solid dome, sleep eyes, open mouth, also in composition, newborn
519	Armand Marseille	ca 1938	"AM", socket or flange neck, solid dome, sleep eyes, open mouth, composition, newborn
520	Armand Marseille	GM 1910	"AM 232", character, solid dome, sleep eyes, open mouth (1938 in composition and composition)
520	Baehr & Proeschild	ca 1910	with and without "K&H", character, painted eyes, closed smiling mouth, for Kley & Hahn

Mold No.	Firm	Date	Description and Identification
521	F.&W. Goebel	ca 1910	shoulder head, glass eyes, open mouth
525	Hermann Kiesewetter	GM 1926	doll with character eyes
525	Baehr & Proeschild	ca 1912	"K&H" or only with mold number, character, solid dome, painted or sleep eyes, grinning, open/closed mouth, for Kley & Hahn
526	Baehr & Proeschild	ca 1912	"K&H", character, painted eyes, closed mouth, for Kley & Hahn
529	Baehr & Proeschild	ca 1912	"B&P" with and without "2025", character, painted eyes, closed mouth
530	Simon & Halbig	ca 1910	"S&H", dolly face, sleep eyes, open mouth
531	Baehr & Proeschild	ca 1912	"K&H" or only with mold number, character, solid dome, painted eyes, open/closed mouth, for Kley & Hahn
535	Baehr & Proeschild	ca 1912	"B&P" in heart, character
536	Baehr & Proeschild	ca 1912	character, painted or glass eyes, open/closed mouth
537	Baehr & Proeschild	ca 1912	"BSW" in heart with "2033", character, sleep eyes, closed mouth, for Bruno Schmidt
539	Baehr & Proeschild	ca 1912	"BSW" in heart with "2023", character, solid dome, painted eyes, closed mouth, for Bruno Schmidt

Mold No.	Firm	Date	Description and Identification
540	Baehr & Proeschild	ca 1912	"BSW" in heart with "2024", character, solid dome, painted eyes, closed mouth
540	Gebr. Eckardt	ca 1935	"GEO", character, baby, glass eyes, open mouth
540	Simon & Halbig	ca 1910	"S&H", dolly face, glass eyes, open mouth
541	Armand Marseille	ca 1930	"GEO", character, baby, for Gebr. Eckhardt
541	Baehr & Proeschild	ca 1912	"WSK", character, solid dome, painted eyes, open/closed mouth, for Wiesenthal, Schindel & Kallenberg
541	Armand Marseille	ca 1926	"AM", newborn, sleep eyes, closed mouth, Oriental
542	Armand Marseille	ca 1926	"AM", newborn, solid dome, flange neck, painted or sleep eyes, open mouth, porcelain or composition
546	Baehr & Proeschild	ca 1912	"K&H", character, glass eyes, closed mouth, for Kley & Hahn
547	Baehr & Proeschild	ca 1912	character, glass eyes, closed mouth
548	Baehr & Proeschild	ca 1912	"K&H", character, solid dome, painted or glass eyes, open/closed mouth with molded tongue, for Kley & Hahn
549	Baehr & Proeschild	ca 1912	"K&H", character, painted eyes, closed mouth, also in celluloid, for Kley & Hahn

Mold No.	Firm	Date	Description and Identification
549	Simon & Halbig	ca 1910	"S&H", dolly face, glass eyes, open mouth, Mulatto
550	Erste Steinbacher Porzellanfabrik	ca 1926	"GH", character, painted eyes, laughing open mouth
550	Simon & Halbig	ca 1910	"S&H", dolly face, sleep eyes, open mouth
550	Armand Marseille	ca 1926	"AM", character, solid dome, sleep eyes, closed mouth
550a	Armand Marseille	ca 1926	"AM DRGM ", character, wig, sleep eyes, closed mouth
551	Armand Marseille	ca 1930	"AM", character, flange neck, baby
551k	Armand Marseille	ca 1930	"AM", character, head, baby
554	Baehr & Proeschild	ca 1912	"K&H", character, glass eyes, open/closed mouth, crying voice, for Kley & Hahn
556	Karl Schirmer	GM 1925	doll head
560	Armand Marseille	GM 1910	"AM 232", character, solid dome, painted eyes, open/closed mouth
560a	Armand Marseille	ca 1926	"AM 232", character, wig, sleep eyes, open mouth
561	Baehr & Proeschild	ca 1912	character, solid dome, glass eyes, open/closed mouth
563	Baehr & Proeschild	ca 1912	"Schneewittchen", character, solid dome, sleep eyes, open/closed mouth, for Kley & Hahn
563	Baehr & Proeschild	ca 1912	"Schneeglöckchen", character, solid dome, sleep eyes, open or open/closed mouth, for Nöckler & Tittel

Mold No.	Firm	Date	Description and Identification
567	Baehr & Proeschild	GM 1911	character, two-face-doll, laughing: glass eyes, open mouth, crying: painted eyes, open/closed mouth, for Kley & Hahn
568	Baehr & Proeschild	ca 1912	"K&H", character, solid dome, sleep eyes, open/closed mouth with molded tongue, smiling, for Kley & Hahn
570	Armand Marseille	GM 1910	"AM 232", shoulder head, dolly face, sleep eyes, open mouth
570	Simon & Halbig	ca 1910	"S&H", dolly face
571	Baehr & Proeschild	ca 1912	"K&H", character, solid dome, glass eyes, open/closed mouth, laughing, big baby, for Kley & Hahn
573	Ernst Heubach	ca 1928	character, sleep eyes, open/closed mouth, molded teeth
580	Armand Marseille	ca 1930	"AM", character
580	Erste Steinbacher Porzellanfabrik	ca 1926	"G&H" (owner Gustav Heubach), character, solid dome, painted eyes, open/closed mouth
581	Baehr & Proeschild	ca 1912	character, solid dome, painted eyes, open/closed mouth
582	Baehr & Proeschild	ca 1914	"Germany", character, solid dome, sleep eyes, open/closed mouth with 2 teeth below
584	Baehr & Proeschild	ca 1914	character, solid dome, sleep eyes, open/closed mouth

Mold No.	Firm	Date	Description and Identification
585	Baehr & Proeschild	ca 1912	"B&P" in heart or "B&P" in crossed sword or only with mold number, character, sleep eyes, open mouth
586	Baehr & Proeschild	ca 1915	character, sleep eyes, open/closed mouth
590	Armand Marseille	ca 1926	"AM DRGM ", character, sleep eyes, open/closed mouth, in composition since 1930
592	Baehr & Proeschild	ca 1912	"BP", character, sleep eyes, open/closed mouth
596	Baehr & Proeschild	ca 1912	"BP", character, solid dome, glass eyes, open/closed mouth
599	Armand Marseille	ca 1928	"AM", Japanese, newborn or with "HvB", newborn, for Hermann von Berg
599	Armand Marseille	ca 1928	"AM", Japanese, newborn or with "HvB", newborn, for Hermann von Berg
600	Simon & Halbig	ca 1912	"S&H", character, sleep eyes, open mouth
600	Unknown	ca 1910	shoulder head, glass eyes, open mouth
604	Baehr & Proeschild	ca 1920	with or without "B&P" with crossed swords, character, sleep eyes, open/closed mouth with twoe molded teeth or open mouth
606	Unknown	ca 1900	"LM", straight neck
607	Simon & Halbig	ca 1912	"S&H", character, sleep eyes, open mouth

Mold No.	Firm	Date	Description and Identification
614	Unknown	ca 1925	newborn, character, solid dome, glass eyes, closed pouty mouth
616	Fritz Bierschenk	GM 1910	"FB", presumably character
616	Simon & Halbig	ca 1915	"S&H", character, sleep eyes, open mouth
619	Baehr & Proeschild	ca 1914	"B&P" with crossed swords, character, solid dome, glass eyes, open mouth
620	Koenig & Wernicke	ca 1938	"K&W", character,
620	Armand Marseille	ca 1925	"Germany ARRANBEE", newborn, solid dome, sleep eyes, open mouth with movable tongue
620	Armand Marseille	GM 1910	"AM 234", character, solid dome, painted eyes, closed mouth, boy
620	Baehr & Proeschild	ca 1914	character, solid dome, sleep eyes, open mouth, also with "GB&C" for Geo.Borgfeldt & Co.
620	Unknown	ca 1935	"PORO", composition
621	Armand Marseille	GM 1910	"AM 234", presumably character
622	Alt, Beck & Gottschalck	ca 1890	dolly face, also as Mulatto
623	Unknown	ca 1935	"Germany", character, molded hair, composition
624	Baehr & Proeschild	ca 1915	"B&P" with crossed swords, character
625	Unknown	ca 1935	"Germany", character, flange neck, composition

Mold No.	Firm	Date	Description and Identification
630	Armand Marseille	GM 1910	"AM 234", character, shoulder head, solid dome, painted eyes, open/closed mouth
630	Alt, Beck & Gottschalck	ca 1880	dolly face, glass eyes, open or closed mouth, often on Jumeau-body
632	Unknown	ca 1935	"PORO", newborn
639	Alt, Beck & Gottschalck	ca 1880	"Germany", shoulder head, solid dome, glass eyes, closed mouth
640	Baehr & Proeschild	GM 1915	presumably character
640a	Armand Marseille	GM 1910	"AM 640a 234", character, shoulder head, painted eyes, closed mouth
641	Baehr & Proeschild	GM 1915	"B&P" with crossed swords, character, sleep eyes, open mouth with tongue
642	Baehr & Proeschild	GM 1915	presumably character
643	Baehr & Proeschild	GM 1915	presumably character
644	Baehr & Proeschild	GM 1915	presumably character
645	Baehr & Proeschild	GM 1915	presumably character
646	Baehr & Proeschild	GM 1915	presumably character
649	Baehr & Proeschild	ca 1915	character, solid dome, painted eyes, closed mouth
660	Baehr & Proeschild	ca 1920	"P&B HARMUS" with crossed swords, character, sleep eyes, open mouth, for Carl Harmus
665	Armand Marseille	ca 1938	"AM", character with molded hair

Mold No.	Firm	Date	Description and Identification
670	Armand Marseille	ca 1925	"AM", shoulder head
678	Baehr & Proeschild	ca 1920	"B&P" or "2099", character, sleep eyes, open mouth, for Bruno Schmidt
680	Armand Marseille	ca 1925	"ARRANBEE", newborn, solid dome, sleep eyes, open mouth
680	Kestner & Comp.	ca 1920	"K&CO K&H" and "266 K&H", character, sleep eyes, open mouth, for Kley & Hahn
686	Baehr & Proeschild	ca 1914	"B&P" in heart, character, googly eyes, closed mouth
692	Baehr & Proeschild	ca 1914	"BSW" in heart, character, sleep eyes, open mouth, for Bruno Schmidt
693	Simon & Halbig	ca 1915	"S&H", character
693	Alt, Beck & Gottschalck	ca 1880	shoulder head, glass eyes, closed mouth
694	Baehr & Proeschild	ca 1915	"BP" in heart, character, googly eyes, closed mouth
696	Alt, Beck & Gottschalck	ca 1880	shoulder head, molded hair, painted eyes, closed mouth
696	Armand Marseille	ca 1930	with and without "AM", flange neck, painted or sleep eyes, open mouth
698	Alt, Beck & Gottschalck	ca 1880	with or without "Germany", shoulder head, glass eyes, open or closed mouth
700	Armand Marseille	ca 1920	"AM", character, sleep eyes, closed mouth

Mold No.	Firm	Date	Description and Identification
700	Unknown	ca 1910	character, painted eyes, closed mouth
700	Kämmer & Reinhardt	ca 1910	character, celluloid, see mold # 100
701	Armand Marseille	ca 1920	"AM", character, sleep eyes, closed mouth
701	Carl Knoll, Böhmen	ca 1900	"CK", dolly face, sleep eyes, open mouth
701	Kämmer & Reinhardt	ca 1910	"K&R", character, celluloid, see mold # 101
707	Baehr & Proeschild	ca 1915	character, googly eyes, closed mouth
709	Simon & Halbig	ca 1887	dolly face, shoulder head, glass eyes, open mouth
710	Armand Marseille	ca 1920	"AM", Indian
711	Armand Marseille	ca 1920	"AM", shoulder head, glass eyes, closed mouth
715	Kämmer & Reinhardt	ca 1912	"K&R", character, celluloid, see mold # 115
716	Kämmer & Reinhardt	ca 1912	"K&R", character, celluloid, see mold # 116
717	Kämmer & Reinhardt	ca 1920	"K&R", character, celluloid, see mold # 117
718	Kämmer & Reinhardt	ca 1920	"K&R", character, celluloid, see mold # 118
719	Kämmer & Reinhardt	ca 1920	"K&R", character, celluloid, see mold # 119

Mold No.	Firm	Date	Description and Identification
719	Simon & Halbig	ca 1886	"SH dep", dolly face, glass eyes, open or closed mouth, also as black doll, often found on Edison-Phonograph-Dolls
720	Kämmer & Reinhardt	ca 1920	"K&R", character, celluloid, see mold # 120
720	Simon & Halbig	GM 1887	"SH dep", shoulder head, expression of a one to two year old child
721	Kämmer & Reinhadt	ca 1920	"K&R", character, celluloid, see mold # 121
725	A. Luge & Co.	GM 1930	South-Sea-Baby
726	Kämmer & Reinhardt	ca 1920	"K&R", character, celluloid, see mold # 126
727	Kämmer & Reinhardt	GM 1914	"K&R", character, celluloid, see mold # 127
728	Kämmer & Reinhardt	GM 1915	"K&R", character, celluloid, see mold # 128
728	Simon & Halbig	GM 1888	"S&H", laughing face, glass eyes, open/closed mouth with molded teeth
729	Simon & Halbig	GM 1888	"S&H", laughing face, glass eyes, open/closed mouth with molded teeth, also as black doll
730	Kämmer & Reinhardt	ca 1920	"K&R", character, celluloid, same mold # 130
733	Koenig & Wernicke	ca 1935	"K&W", character, celluloid
737	Kämmer & Reinhardt	ca 1930	character, celluloid, sleep eyes, open mouth

Mold No.	Firm	Date	Description and Identification
738	Simon & Halbig	GM 1888	"S&H", dolly face
739	Simon & Halbig	GM 1888	"S&H", dolly face, glass eyes, closed or open mouth, also as black doll
740	Simon & Halbig	GM 1888	"S&H", dolly face, shoulder head, solid dome with a hole, glass eyes, closed mouth
740	A. Luge & Co.	GM 1910	character baby
740	Arthur Krauß	GM 1926	new born baby with hair
748	Simon & Halbig	GM 1888	"S&H", dolly face
749	Simon & Halbig	GM 1888	"S&H", dolly face, glass eyes, closed or open mouth
750	Simon & Halbig	GM 1888	"S&H", dolly face, shoulder head, glass eyes, open mouth
750	Armand Marseille	GM 1913	"AM 258", character
755	Kämmer & Reinhardt	ca 1930	newborn, character, sleep eyes, closed mouth, celluloid
758	Simon & Halbig	GM 1888	"S&H", dolly face
759	Simon & Halbig	GM 1888	"S&H", dolly face, glass eyes, open mouth, also as black doll
760	Simon & Halbig	GM 1888	"S&H", dolly face, shoulder head
760	Armand Marseille	ca 1920	"AM", character
768	Simon & Halbig	GM 1888	"S&H", dolly face
769	Simon & Halbig	GM 1888	"S&H", dolly face, also as black doll

Mold No.	Firm	Date	Description and Identification
770	Simon & Halbig	GM 1888	"S&H", dolly face, shoulder head
772	Alt, Beck & Gottschalck	ca 1880	shoulder head, molded hair, painted eyes, closed mouth
772	Simon & Halbig	ca 1888	"DEP", dolly face, sleep eyes, open mouth
773	Kämmer & Reinhardt	ca 1925	character, celluloid
775	Kämmer & Reinhardt	ca 1925	character, celluloid
776	Kämmer & Reinhardt	ca 1925	character, celluloid, Mulatto
777	Kämmer & Reinhardt	ca 1925	character, celluloid, Japanese
777	Rudolf Leschhorn	GM 1928	Charles Lindbergh
778	Koenig & Wernicke	ca 1930	"K&W", character, celluloid
778	Simon & Halbig	GM 1888	"S&H", dolly face
782	Alt, Beck & Gottschalck	ca 1880	dolly face, glass eyes, closed mouth
784	Alt, Beck & Gottschalck	ca 1880	shoulder head, china, molded hair, painted eyes, closed mouth
790	Armand Marseille	ca 1920	"AM", character
800	Armand Marseille	GM 1910	"AM 234", character, sleep eyes, open or open/closed mouth, also with head voice
800	Porzellanfabrik Mengersgereuth	ca 1926	"PM", newborn
800	Unknown	ca 1926	"Germany", newborn

Mold No.	Firm	Date	Description and Identification
800	Sonneberger Porzellanfabrik	ca 1948	"SP" in circle, flange neck, composition, molded hair, sleep eyes, open mouth
800	Carl Harmus	ca 1905	"Harmus", dolly face
800	Kämmer & Reinhardt	ca 1928	character, baby, rubber (see mold # 100)
801	Unknown	ca 1926	"Germany", newborn, sleep eyes, closed mouth
802	Unknown	ca 1900	"W", dolly face
806	Unknown	ca 1880	"TR", dolly face, solid dome with three holes, glass eyes, closed mouth
810	Armand Marseille	ca 1915	"AM", shoulder head, sleep eyes, open/closed mouth
812	Alt, Beck & Gottschalck	ca 1895	dolly face, glass eyes, open mouth
813	Unknown	ca 1880	"TR", dolly face, solid dome with multi holes, glass eyes, closed mouth
814	Unknown	ca 1926	"Germany", character, sleep eyes, open mouth
817	Kämmer & Reinhardt	ca 1928	"K&R", character, rubber, (see mold # 117)
820	Armand Marseille	ca 1915	"AM", character, shoulder head, sleep eyes, open/closed mouth
826	Kämmer & Reinhardt	ca 1928	"K&R", character, rubber, (see mold # 126)

Mold No.	Firm	Date	Description and Identification
828	Kämmer & Reinhardt	ca 1928	"K&R", character, rubber, (see mold # 128)
828	Porzellanfabrik Mengergereuth	ca 1920	"PM", character, molded hair with bow and flowers, painted eyes, open/closed mouth with molded teeth
830	Porzellanfabrik Mengersgereuth	ca 1920	"PM", character
831	Kämmer & Reinhardt	ca 1928	"K&R", character, rubber, (see mold # 131)
837	Simon & Halbig	ca 1880	"S&H", dolly face, for all-bisque-body
842	Unknown	ca 1926	"J.L.Kallus:Copr.Germany", character, solid dome, glass eyes, open mouth, all-bisque, baby Bo Kaye
845	Simon & Halbig	GM 1878	Frozen Charlie (all-bisque)
846	Simon & Halbig	GM 1878	Frozen Charlie (all-bisque)
847	Simon & Halbig	GM 1880	Frozen Charlie (all-bisque)
848	Simon & Halbig	GM 1880	Frozen Charlie (all-bisque)
852	Simon & Halbig	ca 1880	"S&H", dolly face, for all-bisque-body
862	Alt, Beck & Gottschalck	ca 1895	dolly face, glass eyes, closed mouth
866	Alt, Beck & Gottschalck	GM 1895	doll head
867	Alt, Beck & Gottschalck	GM 1895	doll head

Mold No.	Firm	Date	Description and Identification
868	Alt, Beck & Gottschalck	GM 1895	doll head
869	Alt, Beck & Gottschalck	GM 1895	doll head
870	Alt, Beck & Gottschalck	GM 1895	shoulder head, solid dome, glass eyes, closed mouth
871	Heinrich Bätz	GM 1930	character
873	Kämmer & Reinhardt	ca 1928	"K&R", character, rubber, (see mold # 173)
878	Simon & Halbig	ca 1880	"S&H", dolly face, for all-bisque-body
879	Alt, Beck & Gottschalck	ca 1895	shoulder head, sleep eyes, closed mouth
880	Simon & Halbig	ca 1880	"S&H", dolly face, for all-bisque-body
880	Alt, Beck & Gottschalck	ca 1890	shoulder head, molded hair
847	Simon & Halbig	GM 1880	Frozen Charlie (all-bisque)
848	Simon & Halbig	GM 1880	Frozen Charlie (all-bisque)
852	Simon & Halbig	ca 1880	"S&H", dolly face, for all-bisque-body
866	Alt, Beck & Gottschalck	GM 1895	doll head
867	Alt, Beck & Gottschalck	GM 1895	doll head
868	Alt, Beck & Gottschalck	GM 1895	doll head

Mold No.	Firm	Date	Description and Identification
869	Alt, Beck & Gottschalck	GM 1895	doll head
870	Alt, Beck & Gottschalck	GM 1895	shoulder head, glass eyes,
871	Heinrich Bätz	GM 1930	character
873	Kämmer & Reinhardt	ca 1928	"K&R", character, rubber, (see mold # 173)
878	Simon & Halbig	ca 1880	"S&H", dolly face, for all-bisque-body
879	Alt, Beck & Gottschalck	ca 1895	shoulder head, sleep eyes, closed mouth
880	Simon & Halbig	ca 1880	"S&H", dolly face, for all-bisque-body
880	Alt, Beck & Gottschalck	ca 1890	shoulder head, molded hair, glass eyes, closed mouth
881	Simon & Halbig	ca 1880	"S&H", dolly face, for all-bisque-body
882	Dornheim, Koch & Fischer	GM 1892	crossed swords, shoulder head, molded hair, painted features
882	Alt, Beck & Gottschalck	ca 1890	shoulder head, molded hair, glass eyes, closed mouth
886	Simon & Halbig	ca 1880	"S&H", dolly face, for all-bisque-body, also as black doll
886	Theodor Recknagel	GM 1926	"AR Germany LA&S", newborn, sleep eyes, closed or open mouth
887	Simon & Halbig	ca 1880	"S&H", dolly face, for all-bisque-body
888	Geo. Borgfeldt & Co.	GM 1927	character

Mold No.	Firm	Date	Description and Identification
889	Alt, Beck & Gottschalck	ca 1890	shoulder head with molded hair, glass eyes, closed mouth
889	Geo. Borgfeldt & Co.	GM 1927	character
890	Alt, Beck & Gottschalck	ca 1890	shoulder head, molded hair, blond or black, painted eyes, closed mouth
890	Simon & Halbig	ca 1880	"S&H", dolly face, for all-bisque-body
890	Ernst Metzler	ca 1920	"EM", dolly face
890a	Otto Jäger	ca 1922	character
894	Alt, Beck & Gottschalck	ca 1880	shoulder head with molded blue scarf, painted or glass eyes, closed mouth, also without mold number
896	Simon & Halbig	GM 1913	Frozen Charlie with painted or sleep eyes
898	Alt, Beck & Gottschalck	ca 1880	shoulder head with molded hair, painted features, type "Kaiserin Augusta"
898	Simon & Halbig	GM 1913	Frozen Charlie with painted eyes, glass-eyes or sleep eyes
899	Simon & Halbig	GM 1913	Frozen Charlie with painted, glass-eyes, presumably marked with "dep", all bisque
900	Armand Marseille	ca 1920	"AM", character
900	Porzellanfabrik Burggrub	ca 1930	character, baby
900	Kämmer & Reinhardt	ca 1930	"K&R", character, composition (see mold # 100)

Mold No.	Firm	Date	Description and Identification
900	Unknown	ca 1880	"TR", shoulder head, solid dome with little hole, glass eyes, closed mouth
901	Simon & Halbig	GM 1913	Frozen Charlie, with stationary head and arms, or with movable head and arms
901	Kämmer & Reinhardt	ca 1930	"K&R", character, composition (see mold # 101)
904	Porzellanfabrik Mengersgereuth	ca 1920	"PM", character
904	Unknown	ca 1890	dolly face, glass eyes, open mouth
905	Simon & Halbig	ca 1888	"S&H", dolly face, glass eyes, closed mouth
908	Simon & Halbig	ca 1888	"S&H", dolly face, sleep eyes, open or closed mouth
908	Unknown	ca 1880	"TR", dolly face, shoulder head, solid dome, glass eyes, closed mouth
909	Simon & Halbig	ca 1888	"S&H", dolly face, glass eyes, open mouth
911	Alt, Beck & Gottschalck	ca 1890	shoulder head, glass eyes, closed mouth
914	Schoenau & Hoffmeister	ca 1925	"SPBH", character
914	Porzellanfabrik Mengersgereuth	ca 1920	"PM", character, sleep eyes, open mouth
915	Porzellanfabrik Mengersgereuth	ca 1920	character

Mold No.	Firm	Date	Description and Identification
915	Alt, Beck & Gottschalck	ca 1890	shoulder head, glass eyes, closed mouth
916	Alt, Beck & Gottschalck	ca 1890	shoulder head, glass eyes, open/closed mouth
916	Porzellanfabrik Mengergereuth	ca 1920	character, sleep eyes, open mouth
917	Kämmer & Reinhardt	ca 1930	"K&R", character, composition (see mold # 117)
918	Simon & Halbig	ca 1880	"S&H/K&R", dolly face, for all-bisque-body, marked with "918", in all bisque since 1910
919	Simon & Halbig	ca 1888	"S&H", dolly face, glass eyes, closed mouth with space, slightly smiling.
920	Simon & Halbig	ca 1888	"S&H", shoulder head, solid dome, glass eyes, closed mouth with space, slightly smiling
921	Armand Marseille	ca 1920	"AM", shoulder head, sleep eyes, open mouth
921	Kämmer & Reinhardt	ca 1930	"K&R", character, composition, (see mold # 121)
921	Simon & Halbig	ca 1913	"S&H", character, baby, (10 cm)
924	Unknown	ca 1920	flange neck, clown, glass eyes, closed laughing mouth
924	Porzellanfabrik Mengersgereuth	ca 1920	"PM", character, sleep eyes, open mouth
925	Unknown	ca 1900	solid dome, painted eyes, open/closed laughing mouth (presumably for automata)

Mold No.	Firm	Date	Description and Identification
926	Porzellanfabrik Mengersgereuth	GM 1926	character, for Robert Carl
926	Kämmer & Reinhardt	ca 1930	"K&R", character, composition (see mold # 126)
927	Porzellanfabrik Mengersgereuth	GM 1926	character, for Robert Carl
927	Armand Marseille	ca 1920	"AM", character, baby
927	Simon & Halbig	ca 1913	"S&C/S&H", character, for Franz Schmidt & Co., also only with "S&H" produced
928	Porzellanfabrik Mengersgereuth	ca 1926	"PM", character, molded hair with bow, painted features, for Robert Carl
929	Porzellanfabrik Mengersgereuth	GM 1926	character, for Robert Carl
929	Simon & Halbig	ca 1888	"S&H", dolly face, glass eyes, open or closed mouth, also for all-bisque-body
931	Unknown	ca 1925	"KL" newborn, sleep eyes, open mouth
938	Simon & Halbig	ca 1888	dolly face, glass eyes, closed mouth
939	Simon & Halbig	ca 1888	"S&H", dolly face, glass eyes, open or closed mouth
940	Simon & Halbig	ca 1888	"S&H", dolly face, shoulder head, glass eyes, closed mouth
941	Simon & Halbig+	ca 1888	"S&H", shoulder plate, found with "S&H" heads mold # 939

Mold No.	Firm	Date	Description and Identification
949	Simon & Halbig	ca 1888	"S&H", dolly face, glass eyes, open or closed mouth, also as black doll
950	Simon & Halbig	ca 1888	"S&H", dolly face, shoulder head, glass eyes, closed mouth
950	Porzellanfabrik Mengersgereuth	ca 1926	"PM", character, googly eyes, closed mouth
950	Armand Marseille	ca 1920	"AM", character, solid dome, painted eyes, closed mouth
951	Armand Marseille	ca 1920	"AM", character, baby
952	Kämmer & Reinhardt	ca 1930	"K&R", character, composition, black doll
959	Simon & Halbig	ca 1888	"S&H", dolly face, glass eyes, open mouth
966	Armand Marseille	GM 1938	"AM", character, sleep eyes, open mouth, composition
966	Hugo Wiegand	GM 1911	baby
967	Hugo Wiegand	GM 1911	baby
968	Simon & Halbig	GM 1887	"S&H", dolly face, glass eyes, smiling, open mouth
969	Simon & Halbig	GM 1887	"S&H", dolly face, glass eyes, smiling, open mouth, also as black doll
970	Simon & Halbig	GM 1887	"S&H", dolly face, shoulder head, glass eyes, smiling open mouth, also as black doll
970	Armand Marseille	ca 1922	"AM", character, also for Otto Gans produced

Mold No.	Firm	Date	Description and Identification
971	Armand Marseille	GM 1913	"AM" with and without "267", character, sleep eyes, open mouth
971a	Armand Marseille	GM 1913	"AM 267", character, also with voice
972	Armand Marseille	GM 1926	"AM/LA&S", character, sleep eyes, closed mouth, for Louis Amberg & Son
973	Armand Marseille	GM 1926	"AM/LA&S", character, sleep eyes, closed mouth, "Baby Peggy Montgomery", for Louis Amberg & Son
973	Kämmer & Reinhardt	ca 1930	"K&R", newborn, composition (see mold # 173)
974	Alt, Beck & Gottschalck	ca 1890	shoulder head, molded hair, painted or glass eyes, closed mouth
975	Armand Marseille	ca 1922	"AM", character, baby, sleep eyes, open mouth, for Otto Gans
977	Kämmer & Reinhardt	ca 1930	"K&R", composition, Japanese
978	Alt, Beck & Gottschalck	ca 1890	shoulder head, molded hair, glass eyes, closed mouth
979	Simon & Halbig	GM 1887	"S&H", dolly face
980	Armand Marseille	ca 1920	"AM", character, glass eyes, open mouth
982	Armand Marseille	ca 1924	"c 1924 LA&SNY", character, "Baby Peggy Montgomery", for Louis Amberg & Son.
983	Armand Marseille	ca 1924	"LA&SNY", character, shoulder head, "Baby Peggy Montgomery", for Louis Amberg & Son.

Mold No.	Firm	Date	Description and Identification
984	Armand Marseille	ca 1925	"AM", character, baby
985	Armand Marseille	ca 1925	"AM L.A.&S 1924", character, baby, sleep eyes, open mouth, Baby Peggy, for Louis Amberg & Son.
988	Simon & Halbig	GM 1887	"S&H", dolly face
989	Armand Marseille	ca 1925	"SUR Germany", character, sleep eyes, open mouth, for Seyfarth & Reinhardt
989	Simon & Halbig	GM 1887	"S&H", dolly face, glass eyes, closed mouth
990	Alt, Beck & Gottschalck	ca 1890	shoulder head, molded hat and hair, painted features
990	Simon & Halbig	GM 1887	"S&H", dolly face, shoulder head
990	Armand Marseille	ca 1925	"AM", character, baby, also as black doll
991	Verein. Köppelsdf. Porzellanfabriken.	GM 1930	"AM", character, sleep eyes, open mouth
992	Armand Marseille	ca 1930	"AM", character, Our Pet, for Gebr. Eckardt
993	Armand Marseille	ca 1925	"AM JIO c 1926", character, flange neck, sleep eyes, open mouth, "Kiddiejoy"
994	Alt, Beck & Gottschalck	ca 1890	shoulder head, molded cap, painted eyes, closed mouth
995	Armand Marseille	ca 1930	"AM", character, also as black doll, painted bisque

Mold No.	Firm	Date	Description and Identification
995	Armand Marseille	ca 1930	"AM SUR", character, for Seyfarth & Reinhardt
995	Hugo Wiegand	ca 1913	character
996	Alt, Beck & Gottschalck	ca 1890	shoulder head with molded scarf, painted eyes, closed mouth
996	Armand Marseille	ca 1931	"AM", character, baby, painted bisque
997	Armand Marseille	ca 1925	"AM", character, Kiddiejoy
990	Armand Marseille	ca 1925	"AM", character, baby, also as black doll
991	Verein. Köppelsdf. Porzellanfabriken	GM 1930	"AM", character, sleep eyes, open mouth
992	Armand Marseille	ca 1930	"AM", character, Our Pet, for Gebr. Eckardt
993	Armand Marseille	ca 1925	"AM", character, Kiddiejoy
995	Armand Marseille	ca 1930	"AM", character, also as black doll, painted bisque
995	Armand Marseille	ca 1930	"AM SUR", character, for Seyfarth & Reinhardt
995	Hugo Wiegand	ca 1913	character
996	Armand Marseille	ca 1931	"AM", character, baby, painted bisque
997	Armand Marseille	ca 1925	"AM", character, Kiddiejoy
998	Alt, Beck & Gottschalck	ca 1890	shoulder head, with molded plaits and hat, painted eyes, closed mouth

Mold No.	Firm	Date	Description and Identification
1000	Simon & Halbig	GM 1887	"S&H", dolly face, shoulder head
1000	Alt, Beck & Gottschalck	ca 1890	shoulder head, china or bisque molded hair, blond or black, painted features
1000	Hermann Steiner	ca 1925	"HS", character
1000	Unknown	ca 1890	dolly face, sleep eyes, open mouth, also as black doll
1001	Wagner & Zetsche	GM 1915	doll head
1001	Alt, Beck & Gottschalck	ca 1900	shoulder head, dolly face, sleep eyes, open mouth
1001	Fritz Lutz	GM 1926	doll head
1002	Fritz Lutz	GM 1926	doll head
1002	Unknown	ca 1925	"Germany", newborn, glass eyes, closed mouth, Oriental
1002	Alt, Beck & Gottschalck	ca 1890	shoulder head, molded hair, painted eyes, closed mouth
1003	Fritz Lutz	GM 1926	doll head
1004	Fritz Lutz	GM 1926	doll head
1005	Geo. Borgfeldt & Co.	GM 1929	"1420", character, Bonnie Babe
1007	Fritz Lutz	GM 1926	doll head
1008	Simon & Halbig	GM 1889	"S&H", dolly face
1008	Alt, Beck & Gottschalck	ca 1890	shoulder head, bisque or china, molded hair, painted or glass eyes, closed mouth

Mold No.	Firm	Date	Description and Identification
1009	Alt, Beck & Gottschalck	ca 1890	"dep", dolly face, glass eyes, open mouth
1009	Simon & Halbig	GM 1889	"S&H", dolly face, glass eyes, open or closed mouth, also as black doll
1010	Simon & Halbig	GM 1889	"S&H", dolly face, shoulder head, glass eyes, open mouth or head on shoulder plate with glass eyes, closed mouth
1018	Simon & Halbig	GM 1890	"S&H", laughing face
1019	Simon & Halbig	GM 1890	"S&H", laughing face, often on Ondine-swimming-doll
1020	Simon & Halbig	GM 1890	"S&H", laughing face, shoulder head
1020	Alt, Beck & Gottschalck	ca 1890	shoulder head, molded hair with pearl ribbon, painted eyes, closed mouth
1024	Alt, Beck & Gottschalck	ca 1890	shoulder head
1026	Alt, Beck & Gottschalck	ca 1890	shoulder head, molded cap, painted eyes, closed mouth
1028	Alt, Beck & Gottschalck	ca 1890	shoulder head, molded hair, painted eyes, closed mouth
1029	Simon & Halbig	ca 1890	"S&H DRP 56562", dolly face with sleep eyesmechanism, open mouth
1030	Alt, Beck & Gottschalck	ca 1890	shoulder head, china, molded black hair, painted features, type Kaiserin Augusta

Mold No.	Firm	Date	Description and Identification
1032	Alt, Beck & Gottschalck	ca 1890	shoulder head, glass eyes, closed mouth
1038	Simon & Halbig	GM 1891	"S&H", dolly face, glass eyes, open mouth
1039	Simon & Halbig	GM 1891	"S&H", dolly face, sleep eyes, open mouth, also as black doll (stamped "Wimpern geschützt")
1040	Simon & Halbig	GM 1891	"S&H", dolly face, shoulder head, sleep eyes, open mouth
1041	Simon & Halbig	GM 1891	"S&H", shoulder plate, found with "S&H" heads mold number 939 or 1009 or 1079
1044	Alt, Beck & Gottschalck	ca 1890	shoulder head, painted or glass eyes, closed mouth
1046	Alt, Beck & Gottschalck	ca 1890	shoulder head, molded hair, painted or glass eyes, closed mouth
1046	Louis Reber	ca 1924	"DRGM 897388", head from rubber, painted eyes, open/closed mouth
1049	Simon & Halbig	ca 1891	"S&H", dolly face, glass eyes, open mouth
1054	Alt, Beck & Gottschalck	ca 1890	shoulder head with molded cap, glass eyes, closed mouth
1056	Alt, Beck & Gottschalck	ca 1890	shoulder head, molded hair, china or bisque, painted eyes, closed mouth
1058	Simon & Halbig	GM 1891	"S&H", dolly face
1059	Simon & Halbig	GM 1891	"S&H", dolly face, glass eyes, open mouth

Mold No.	Firm	Date	Description and Identification
1060	Simon & Halbig	GM 1891	"S&H", dolly face, shoulder head
1061	Simon & Halbig	GM 1891	"S&H", shoulder plate
1062	Alt, Beck & Gottschalck	ca 1890	shoulder head, molded hair, painted or glass eyes, closed mouth
1064	Alt, Beck & Gottschalck	ca 1890	shoulder head, molded hair, painted eyes, closed mouth
1068	Simon & Halbig	GM 1892	"S&H", dolly face
1069	Simon & Halbig	GM 1892	"S&H", dolly face
1070	J.D. Kestner jr.	GM 1914	"Hilda", character, solid dome, sleep eyes, open mouth with tongue
1070	Simon & Halbig	GM 1892	"S&H", dolly face, shoulder head
1070	Koenig & Wernicke	ca 1915	"K&W", character, sleep eyes, open/closed mouth
1078	Simon & Halbig	GM 1892	"S&H", dolly face, glass eyes, open mouth, also as black doll
1079	Simon & Halbig	GM 1892	"S&H", as - or shoulder head, dolly face, sleep eyes, open mouth
1080	Simon & Halbig	GM 1892	"S&H", dolly face, shoulder head
1086	Alt, Beck & Gottschalck	ca 1890	shoulder head, molded blond or black hair, painted eyes, closed mouth, china or in bisque with glass eyes
1088	Alt, Beck & Gottschalck	ca 1890	shoulder head, molded hair, painted eyes, closed mouth

Mold No.	Firm	Date	Description and Identification
1092	Alt, Beck & Gottschalck	ca 1890	shoulder head, molded hair, painted eyes, closed mouth, type Kaiserin Augusta
1098	Simon & Halbig	GM 1893	"S&H", dolly face, Chinese
1099	Simon & Halbig	GM 1893	"S&H", dolly face, Chinese
1100	Catterfelder Puppenfabrik	ca 1908	dolly face, sleep eyes, open mouth
1108	Simon & Halbig	GM 1893	"S&H", dolly face
1109	Simon & Halbig	GM 1893	"S&H", dolly face
1110	Simon & Halbig	GM 1893	"S&H", dolly face, shoulder head
1121	Alt, Beck & Gottschalck	ca 1890	shoulder head, solid dome, glass eyes, closed mouth
1123	Alt, Beck & Gottschalck	ca 1893	"made in Germany", shoulder head, glass eyes, open mouth
1127	Alt, Beck & Gottschalck	ca 1893	shoulder head, glass eyes, closed mouth
1129	Simon & Halbig	ca 1893	"S&H", dolly face, Oriental
1139	Simon & Halbig	ca 1893	"S&H", lady
1142	Alt, Beck & Gottschalck	ca 1890	shoulder head, china porcelain, molded hair, painted eyes, closed mouth
1148	Simon & Halbig	GM 1894	"S&H", dolly face
1149	Simon & Halbig	GM 1894	"S&H", dolly face
1150	Simon & Halbig	GM 1894	"S&H", dolly face, shoulder head

Mold No.	Firm	Date	Description and Identification
1152	Alt, Beck & Gottschalck	GM 1885	"dep", dolly face, glass eyes, open mouth
1153	Alt, Beck & Gottschalck	GM 1885	doll head
1154	Alt, Beck & Gottschalck	ca 1890	shoulder head, dolly face
1158	Simon & Halbig	GM 1894	"S&H", dolly face
1159	Simon & Halbig	GM 1894	"S&H", dolly face, glass eyes, open mouth, named Gibson Girl
1160	Simon & Halbig	GM 1894	"S&H", dolly face, shoulder head, glass eyes, closed mouth, known as "Little Woman"
1170	Simon & Halbig	ca 1895	"S&H", dolly face, shoulder head, glass eyes, open mouth
1170	Alt, Beck & Gottschalck	GM 1888	doll head
1171	Alt, Beck & Gottschalck	GM 1888	doll head
1172	Alt, Beck & Gottschalck	GM 1888	doll head
1173	Alt, Beck & Gottschalck	GM 1888	doll head
1174	Alt, Beck & Gottschalck	GM 1888	doll head
1175	Alt, Beck & Gottschalck	GM 1888	doll head
1176	Alt, Beck & Gottschalck	GM 1888	doll head

Mold No.	Firm	Date	Description and Identification
1177	Alt, Beck & Gottschalck	GM 1888	doll head
1180	Simon & Halbig	ca 1898	"S&H/S&C", dolly face, shoulder head, sleep eyes, open mouth, for Franz Schmidt & Co.
1180	Heinrich Graeser	GM 1890	jointed doll from bisque-porcelain
1199	Simon & Halbig	ca 1898	"S&H", dolly face, glass eyes, open mouth, Oriental
1200	Catterfelder Puppenfabrik	ca 1908	dolly face, sleep eyes, open mouth
1200	Unknown	ca 1900	"MS", dolly face
1210	Alt, Beck & Gottschalck	ca 1890	shoulder head, molded hair, painted or glass eyes, closed mouth
1211	Alt, Beck & Gottschalck	ca 1890	shoulder head, molded hair, painted or glass eyes, closed mouth
1214	Alt, Beck & Gottschalck	ca 1890	shoulder head, china or bisque, painted features
1218	Alt, Beck & Gottschalck	ca 1890	shoulder head with molded curles, painted features
1222	Alt, Beck & Gottschalck	ca 1890	shoulder head, molded hair, painted eyes, closed mouth
1226	Bruno Schmidt	GM 1926	doll head, celluloid, molded bobbed hair and painted eyes, open/closed mouth
1226	Alt, Beck & Gottschalck	ca 1890	shoulder head with molded short hair, painted features
1228	Geo. Borgfeldt & Co.	GM 1902	humorous doll group

Mold No.	Firm	Date	Description and Identification
1234	Alt, Beck & Gottschalck	GM 1899	"DEP", dolly face, shoulder head, solid dome, glass eyes, closed mouth
1235	Alt, Beck & Gottschalck	GM 1899	"DEP GERMANY", dolly face, shoulder head, glass eyes, open mouth
1236	Alt, Beck & Gottschalck	GM 1899	dolly face
1237	Alt, Beck & Gottschalck	GM 1899	dolly face
1246	Simon & Halbig	ca 1898	"S&H", dolly face
1248	Simon & Halbig	GM 1898	"S&H", dolly face, also as black doll
1249	Simon & Halbig	GM 1898	"S&H", dolly face with and without "Santa", for Hamburger & Co.
1250	Simon & Halbig	GM 1898	"S&H", dolly face, shoulder head
1250	Franz Schmidt & Co.	ca 1902	"FS&C" or "S&C", dolly face, sleep eyes, open mouth
1250	Alt, Beck & Gottschalck	ca 1899	"Germany", dolly face, shoulder head, glass eyes, open mouth
1253	Alt, Beck & Gottschalck	ca 1899	shoulder head with molded hair, glass eyes, closed mouth
1253	Franz Schmidt & Co.	ca 1902	dolly face
1254	Alt, Beck & Gottschalck	ca 1899	dolly face, shoulder head, molded hair, glass eyes, closed mouth
1255	Franz Schmidt & Co.	ca 1912	"F.S.&Co. Dep", character, solid dome, open nostril, open mouth, also as black doll

Mold No.	Firm	Date	Description and Identification
1257	Franz Schmidt & Co.	ca 1912	character, solid dome, molded hair, sleep eyes, open mouth
1259	Franz Schmidt & Co.	ca 1912	"FS&Co", character, sleep eyes, open nostril, open mouth
1260	Simon & Halbig	ca 1899	"S&H" or "Halbig", shoulder head, dolly face
1260	Alt, Beck & Gottschalck	GM 1892	"Germany Dep", shoulder head, dolly face, glass eyes, open mouth
1261	Alt, Beck & Gottschalck	GM 1892	doll head
1262	Franz Schmidt & Co.	ca 1912	"FS&Co", character, painted eyes, closed mouth
1263	Franz Schmidt & Co.	ca 1912	"FS&Co", character, painted eyes, closed mouth
1266	Franz Schmidt & Co.	ca 1912	"FS&Co", character, solid dome, painted eyes, closed mouth
1267	Franz Schmidt & Co.	ca 1912	"FS&Co", character, solid dome, painted eyes, closed mouth
1268	Alt, Beck & Gottschalck	GM 1892	"Germany Dep.No", dolly face, glass eyes, open mouth
1269	Simon & Halbig	ca 1899	"S&H", dolly face
1269	Alt, Beck & Gottschalck	GM 1892	doll head
1270	Alt, Beck & Gottschalck	GM 1892	doll head
1270	Franz Schmidt & Co.	GM 1910	character, solid dome, painted eyes, open/closed mouth with molded tongue, 2 teeth upper

Mold No.	Firm	Date	Description and Identification
1271	Alt, Beck & Gottschalck	GM 1892	doll head
1271	Franz Schmidt & Co.	GM 1910	"FS&Co.Deponiert", character, solid dome, sleep eyes, closed mouth
1272	Franz Schmidt & Co.	GM 1910	"FS&Co." with and without "Deponiert", solid dome or wig, sleep eyes, open nostril, open mouth, movable tongue, also as black doll
1274	Franz Schmidt & Co.	GM 1911	character
1278	Alt, Beck & Gottschalck	GM 1892	doll head
1278	Simon & Halbig	GM 1899	"S&H DEP", dolly face, sleep eyes, open mouth
1279	Alt, Beck & Gottschalck	GM 1892	doll head
1279	Simon & Halbig	GM 1899	"S&H", dolly face, sleep eyes, open mouth
1280	Simon & Halbig	GM 1899	"S&H", with and without "Columbia", dolly face, shoulder head, for C.M. Bergmann
1286	Franz Schmidt & Co.	ca 1915	character, molded hair with blue hairbow, glass eyes, open laughing mouth
1287	Franz Schmidt & Co.	ca 1915	character, painted eyes, open/closed mouth with 2 teeth
1288	Alt, Beck & Gottschalck	ca 1890	shoulder head with molded hair, glass eyes, closed mouth

Mold No.	Firm	Date	Description and Identification
1289	Simon & Halbig	GM 1901	doll head
1290	Alt, Beck & Gottschalck	GM 1893	"made in Germany dep", dolly face, shoulder head, glass eyes, open mouth
1291	Alt, Beck & Gottschalck	GM 1893	doll head
1293	Simon & Halbig	ca 1912	"FS&Co", character, for Franz Schmidt & Co.
1294	Simon & Halbig	ca 1912	"S&H", also only with "Germany", character, baby, also as black doll
1295	Simon & Halbig	ca 1912	"FS&Co" or only "S&H", character, sleep eyes, open nostril, open mouth, for Franz Schmidt & Co.
1296	Simon & Halbig	ca 1912	"FS&Co" with and without "1310", character, sleep eyes, open nostril, open mouth, for Franz Schmidt & Co.
1296	Simon & Halbig	ca 1912	"PO", composition, otherwise as before ca 1930
1297	Simon & Halbig	ca 1912	"FS&Co", character, solid dome, sleep eyes, open nostril, open mouth, movable tongue, Franz Schmidt & Co.
1298	Simon & Halbig	ca 1912	"FS&Co", character, for Franz Schmidt & Co.
1299	Simon & Halbig	ca 1912	"S&H" or "FS&Co", character, for Franz Schmidt & Co.
1300	Simon & Halbig	ca 1902	"S&H DEP", dolly face, glass eyes with eye lashes of thread, open mouth, often as French automata

Mold No.	Firm	Date	Description and Identification
1301	Simon & Halbig	ca 1902	"S&H DEP", dolly face, glass eyes with eye lashes of thread, closed mouth, black doll
1302	Simon & Halbig	ca 1902	"S&H DEP", dolly face, glass eyes, closed mouth, black doll
1303	Simon & Halbig	ca 1902	"S&H DEP", expressive lady face, glass eyes, eye lashes of thread, closed mouth
1303	Simon & Halbig	ca 1912	"S&H", expressive Indian-face, painted or glass eyes, closed mouth, colored porcelain
1304	Simon & Halbig	ca 1902	"S&H", expressive face, big glass eyes, closed mouth
1305	Simon & Halbig	ca 1902	"S&H", expressive face, big glass eyes, long nose, open/closed laughing mouth
1307	Unknown	ca 1926	"124 Germany baby Bo-Kaye", character, solid dome with molded hair, sleep eyes, open mouth
1307	Simon & Halbig	ca 1902	lady face, glass eyes, eye lashes of thread, closed mouth
1308	Simon & Halbig	ca 1902	"S&H E", dolly face, glass eyes, closed mouth
1308	Simon & Halbig	ca 1902	"S&H D", man face, glass eyes, closed mouth, dirty colored faces (charcoal burner)
1308	Simon & Halbig	ca 1902	"S&H D", man face, glass eyes, closed mouth with molded teeth and molded moustache
1308	Simon & Halbig	ca 1902	"S&H D", solid dome, glass eyes, closed mouth

Mold No.	Firm	Date	Description and Identification
1309	Simon & Halbig	ca 1905	"L", dolly face, sleep eyes
1310	Simon & Halbig	ca 1905	"S&C Simon & Halbig", dolly face, for Franz Schmidt & Co.
1310	Simon & Halbig	ca 1905	"FS&C Simon & Halbig" with and without "1296", dolly face, for Franz Schmidt & Co.
1319	Alt, Beck & Gottschalck	ca 1910	character, solid dome, painted eyes, open/closed mouth
1321	Alt, Beck & Gottschalck	ca 1910	"ABG", character, solid dome, painted eyes, open/closed mouth or with wig, sleep eyes, open mouth
1321	Alt, Beck & Gottschalck	ca 1910	"WSK", same as before, for Wiesenthal, Schindel & Kallenberg
1321	Armand Marseille	ca 1935	character, for Hugo Wiegand
1322	Alt, Beck & Gottschalck	GM 1910	"AB&G" with or without "DRGM ", character, solid dome, painted or glass eyes, open/closed mouth or with sleep eyes, open mouth, movable tongue, open crown for wig
1325	Franz Schmidt & Co.	ca 1930	"FS&Co. Germany", character, black doll, composition
1326	Alt, Beck & Gottschalck	GM1912	"DRGM 520942", character, sleep eyes, open mouth
1328	Franz Schmidt & Co.	ca 1930	character, black doll, flirting eyes, closed mouth, composition
1329	Simon & Halbig	ca 1910	"S&H", dolly face, Oriental
1330	Armand Marseille	ca 1935	"AM Köppelsdorf", character, glass eyes, open mouth

Mold No.	Firm	Date	Description and Identification
1332	Keramisches Werk	ca 1932	"KWG", flange neck, character
1333	Armand Marseille	ca 1935	"AM Köppelsdorf", character, glass eyes, open mouth
1339	Simon & Halbig	ca 1908	"S&H" with and without "L.L.&S", dolly face, sleep eyes, open mouth, for Louis Lindner & Söhne
1340	Simon & Halbig	ca 1912	"S&H", character, googly eyes, closed mouth
1342	Alt, Beck & Gottschalck	ca 1912	"ABG", character, sleep eyes, open mouth
1343	Alt, Beck & Gottschalck	ca 1912	"ABG", character
1348	Simon & Halbig	ca 1910	"S&H Dressel", dolly face, Jutta-doll, for Cuno & Otto Dressel
1349	Simon & Halbig	ca 1910	"S&H Dressel", dolly face, Jutta-doll, also as black doll, for Cuno & Otto Dressel
1351	Simon & Halbig	ca 1913	"HWW", character, for Hugo Wiegand
1352	Alt, Beck & Gottschalck	ca 1912	character, sleep eyes, open mouth
1353	Alt, Beck & Gottschalck	ca 1912	character, sleep eyes, open mouth
1353	Armand Marseille	ca 1935	"AM", newborn, composition
1357	Alt, Beck & Gottschalck	ca 1912	"ABG", character, solid dome with molded hair, painted or glass eyes or with wig, open mouth

Mold No.	Firm	Date	Description and Identification
1357	Seyfarth & Reinhardt	ca 1925	"SUR" in circle, character, flange neck
1358	Simon & Halbig	ca 1910	"S&H", dolly face, glass eyes, open mouth, black doll or Mulatto
1358	Alt, Beck & Gottschalck	ca 1912	character, molded hair with ribbon and flowers, painted eyes, open mouth
1359	Alt, Beck & Gottschalck	ca 1912	"ABG", character
1360	Alt, Beck & Gottschalck	ca 1912	"ABG", character, sleep eyes, open mouth
1361	Alt, Beck & Gottschalck	ca 1912	"ABG", character, sleep eyes, open mouth
1362	Alt, Beck & Gottschalck	ca 1912	"ABG", character, sleep eyes, open mouth, also in composition
1363	Alt, Beck & Gottschalck	ca 1912	character, shoulder head, sleep eyes, open mouth
1366	Alt, Beck & Gottschalck	ca 1914	"ABG made in Germany", character
1367	Alt, Beck & Gottschalck	ca 1914	character
1368	Alt, Beck & Gottschalck	ca 1914	character
1368	Simon & Halbig	ca 1910	"S&H", dolly face, glass eyes, open mouth, black doll
1369	Grace & S.Putnam	ca 1925	Bye-Lo-Baby, painted or glass eyes, closed mouth

Mold No.	Firm	Date	Description and Identification
1369	Armand Marseille	ca 1930	"AM", character, glass eyes, open mouth
1370	Simon & Halbig	ca 1915	"S&H", character, also in composition
1370	Simon & Halbig	ca 1915	"KWG", after 1930 Keramische Werkstätten Gräfenhain
1370	Armand Marseille	ca 1938	with and without "AM", newborn, painted eyes, open mouth, composition
1373	Alt, Beck & Gottschalck	ca 1920	character
1374	Armand Marseille	ca 1930	"Florodora", dolly face with fur brows
1375	Alt, Beck & Gottschalck	ca 1920	character
1376	Alt, Beck & Gottschalck	ca 1920	character
1376	Schützmeister & Quendt	ca 1920	"SQ", character
1377	Unknown	ca 1915	Kewpie flange neck
1385	Simon & Halbig	ca 1910	"S&H", shoulder head, glass eyes, closed mouth, lady
1388	Simon & Halbig	ca 1910	"S&H", expressive characterhead, glass eyes with eye lashes of thread, open/closed smiling mouth, molded teeth

Mold No.	Firm	Date	Description and Identification
1394	Alt, Beck & Gottschalck	ca 1926	"Copr.by JL Kallus", character, flange neck, solid dome, sleep eyes, open mouth, for Geo. Borgfeldt & Co.
1397	Simon & Halbig	ca 1915	"S&H" or with "FS&Co". for Franz Schmidt & Co., character, sleep eyes, open mouth
1398	Simon & Halbig	ca 1910	"S&H", expressive dolly face, glass eyes, eye lashes of thread, laughing mouth, molded teeth, tiny open mouth
1400	Robert Carl Nachf.	GM 1926	"Germany", character, flange neck, solid dome, sleep eyes, closed mouth
1400	Franz Schmidt & Co.	ca 1930	"FS&Co.", character, sleep eyes, open mouth, composition
1400	Schoenau & Hoffmeister	GM 1903	"SPBH", dolly face, shoulder head
1401	Robert Carl Nachf.	GM 1926	character, baby
1402	Alt, Beck & Gottschalck	ca 1925	character
1420	Alt, Beck & Gottschalck	ca 1925	character
1426	Simon & Halbig	ca 1914	"S&H", character, baby
1428	Simon & Halbig	ca 1914	character, sleep eyes, open/closed mouth
1429	Simon & Halbig	ca 1914	"S&H" with and without "Santa", glass eyes, open mouth, for Hamburger & Co.

Mold No.	Firm	Date	Description and Identification
1431	Unknown	ca 1912	character, solid dome, glass eyes, laughing , open mouth
1432	Alt, Beck & Gottschalck	ca 1925	"Albego", character, composition
1448	Simon & Halbig	ca 1914	"S&H", character, sleep eyes, closed mouth
1465	Simon & Halbig	ca 1914	"S&H", character, glass eyes, closed mouth
1468	Simon & Halbig	ca 1920	"S&H", dolly face, glass eyes, closed mouth, flapperdoll, for Cuno & Otto Dressel
1469	Simon & Halbig	ca 1920	"S&H", dolly face, glass eyes, closed mouth, flapperdoll, for Cuno & Otto Dressel
1478	Simon & Halbig	ca 1920	"S&H", character, glass eyes, closed mouth
1485	Simon & Halbig	ca 1920	"S&H", character, glass eyes, closed mouth
1488	Simon & Halbig	ca 1920	"S&H", character, glass eyes, open or open/closed mouth
1489	Simon & Halbig	ca 1925	"S&H Erika", character, sleep eyes, open mouth, presumably for Carl Hartmann
1496	Simon & Halbig	ca 1920	"S&H", lady face
1498	Simon & Halbig	ca 1920	character, solid dome, painted or sleep eyes, open/closed mouth
1500	Unknown	ca 1900	shoulder head, dolly face, glass eyes, open mouth
1514	Theodor Degenring	GM 1890	girlhead

Mold No.	Firm	Date	Description and Identification
1527	Simon & Halbig	ca 1925	"S&H", character, glass eyes, closed mouth
1550	Unknown	ca 1920	character, glass eyes, open/closed mouth
1563	Theodor Degenring	GM 1890	doll head
1565	Geo. Borgfeldt & Co.	GM 1925	"R", doll head
1566	Theodor Degenring	GM 1890	doll head
1569	Theodor Degenring	GM 1890	doll head
1571	Theodor Degenring	GM 1890	doll head
1601	Heinrich Liebermann	GM 1927	presumably "Haliso", doll head from papermaché
1616	Simon & Halbig	ca 1928	"S&H", character, baby, also in composition
1700	Wagner & Zetsche	ca 1920	"W.Z.", character, flange neck, solid dome, molded hair, painted eyes, closed mouth, from Haralit (= composition)
1728	Kämmer & Reinhardt	ca 1925	celluloid, same as mold # 128, produced from turtle-mark
1748	Simon & Halbig	ca 1928	"S&H", character, baby, composition
1776	Cuno & Otto Dressel	ca 1925	"CD dep", dolly face, shoulder head, glass eyes, open mouth
1800	Schoenau & Hoffmeister	ca 1903	"SPBH", dolly face

Mold No.	Firm	Date	Description and Identification
1813	Unknown	ca 1905	dolly face, shoulder head, glass eyes, closed mouth
1848	Simon & Halbig	ca 1920	dolly face, Jutta-doll, for Cuno & Otto Dressel
1849	Simon & Halbig	ca 1920	dolly face, Jutta-doll, for Cuno & Otto Dressel
1890	Armand Marseille	ca 1890	"AM", dolly face, shoulder head
1892	Armand Marseille	ca 1892	"AM", dolly face, shoulder head
1893	Armand Marseille	GM 1892	"AM COD 93 dep", dolly face, shoulder head, for Cuno & Otto Dressel
1894	Armand Marseille	ca 1894	"AM" with or without "DEP", dolly face, also as black doll
1895	Armand Marseille	ca 1895	"AM", dolly face, shoulder head
1895	Moritz Resek	ca 1895	"MR 175", dolly face
1896	Armand Marseille	ca 1896	"AM", dolly face, shoulder head, also for Cuno & Otto Dressel
1897	Armand Marseille	ca 1897	"AM", dolly face, head
1898	Armand Marseille	ca 1898	"AM", dolly face, shoulder head, also for Cuno & Otto Dressel
1899	Armand Marseille	ca 1899	"AM", dolly face, shoulder head
1899	Peter Scherf	ca 1899	"PSch", dolly face, shoulder head
1899	Wenzel Prouza	ca 1899	"WEP", dolly face
1900	Armand Marseille	ca 1900	"AM", dolly face

Mold No.	Firm	Date	Description and Identification
1900	Ernst Heubach	ca 1900	with horseshoe, dolly face
1900	Schoenau & Hoffmeister	ca 1900	"AS" or "SH" and "PB" in star, dolly face, glass eyes, open mouth, for Arthur Schoenau
1900	Plass & Roesner	ca 1910	"PR", dolly face, also as black doll
1900	Unknown	ca 1900	"No", shoulder head, molded hair, painted eyes, closed mouth
1901	Armand Marseille	ca 1901	"AM", dolly face, shoulder head
1901	Peter Scherf	ca 1901	"PSch", dolly face, shoulder head
1901	Ernst Heubach	ca 1901	with horseshoe, dolly face, shoulder head
1902	Armand Marseille	ca 1902	"AM", dolly face, shoulder head
1902	Peter Scherf	ca 1902	"PSch", dolly face, shoulder head
1902	Ernst Heubach	ca 1902	with horseshoe, dolly face, shoulder head
1902	Unknown	ca 1902	dolly face, glass eyes, open mouth
1903	Armand Marseille	ca 1903	"AM", dolly face, shoulder head
1903	Adolf Prouza	ca 1910	"AP", dolly face
1903	Pollack & Hoffmann	ca 1903	"P&H", dolly face
1904	Schoenau & Hoffmeister	ca 1904	"SPBH", dolly face
1904	Erste Steinbacher Porzellanfabrik	ca 1925	"GH", dolly face

Mold No.	Firm	Date	Description and Identification
1904	Pollack & Hoffmann	ca 1904	"P&H", dolly face
1904	A.C. Anger	ca 1920	"AeM", dolly face
1904	A.C. Anger	ca 1920	"Eduardo Juan", dolly face
1905	Armand Marseille	ca 1905	"AM", dolly face, shoulder head
1906	Ernst Heubach	ca 1906	with horseshoe, dolly face, shoulder head
1906	Schoenau & Hoffmeister	ca 1906	"SPBH", dolly face
1906	Carl Knoll	ca 1906	dolly face, glass eyes, open mouth
1907	Theodor Recknagel	GM 1910	"DEP RA", dolly face
1907	Theodor Pohl	ca 1907	"TP", dolly face
1907	Plass & Roesner	ca 1907	"P&R", dolly face
1909	Schoenau & Hoffmeister	ca 1909	"SPBH", dolly face
1909	Armand Marseille	ca 1909	"AM", dolly face, shoulder head
1909	Ernst Heubach	ca 1909	with horseshoe, dolly face, shoulder head
1909	Theodor Recknagel	ca 1910	"DEP RA", dolly face, glass eyes, open mouth
1910	Plass & Roesner Buchauer Porzellanfabrik	ca 1910	"B.P. made in Austria", dolly face, glass eyes, open mouth
1910	Ernst Winkler	ca 1910	"W", dolly face

Mold No.	Firm	Date	Description and Identification
1910	Unknown	ca 1910	"Taft", dolly face, glass eyes, open mouth
1912	Simon & Halbig	ca 1912	"S&H Jutta", dolly face, for Cuno & Otto Dressel
1912	Unknown	ca 1912	"Germany", dolly face, sleep eyes, open mouth
1913	Plass & Roesner	ca 1913	"PR ROMA", dolly face
1913	Heinrich Bätz	GM 1913	doll head
1914	Simon & Halbig	ca 1914	"S&H" with and without "Jutta", character, for Cuno & Otto Dressel
1914	Louis Amberg & Son	ca 1914	"LA&S G45520" newborn, glass eyes, closed mouth
1914	Theodor Recknagel	ca 1914	"Dep RA", dolly face
1914	Heinrich Bätz	GM 1913	doll head
1914	Armand Marseille	ca 1914	"A.M. Duchess", dolly face, for Geo. Borgfeldt
1914	Unknown	ca 1914	"Germany B", dolly face, sleep eyes, open mouth
1916	Simon & Halbig	ca 1925	"S&H", character, composition
1916	C.M. Bergmann	ca 1916	dolly face, sleep eyes
1919	Schoenau & Hoffmeister	ca 1919	"SH PB" im Star, "Carmencita", dolly face, sleep eyes, open mouth
1920	Simon & Halbig	ca 1920	"S&H Jutta", character, for Cuno & Otto Dressel

Mold No.	Firm	Date	Description and Identification
1920	August Möller & Sohn	ca 1920	"Amuso", character
1922	Ernst Heubach	ca 1922	"Jutta- baby Dressel", character, sleep eyes, open mouth, for Cuno & Otto Dressel
1923	Schoenau & Hoffmeister	ca 1923	"SH PB" or with "M", character, sleep eyes, open mouth, for Ma.E. Maar
1924	E.I. Horsman	ca 1924	"c 1924 by E.I.Horsman made in Germany", character, little glass eyes, closed mouth, "Tynie baby"
1924	Theodor Recknagel	ca 1924	"RA", character, newborn, glass eyes, closed mouth
1924	Hermann Pensky	ca 1924	"Hannelore PH", character, sleep eyes, open mouth
1930	Schoenau & Hoffmeister	ca 1930	"Porzellanfabrik Burggrub Das lachende Baby", character, sleep eyes, open laughing mouth
2000	Nikolaus Oberender	ca 1911	"NO", character, shoulder head, solid dome, painted eyes, closed mouth
2000	Armand Marseille	GM 1895	dolly face
2010	Nikolaus Oberender	ca 1911	"NO", character, shoulder head, solid dome, painted eyes, closed mouth
2010	Armand Marseille	GM 1896	"AM", dolly face
2015	Armand Marseille	GM 1896	"W" with Anker, dolly face, shoulder head, glass eyes, closed mouth, presumably for Louis Wolf & Co.

Mold No.	Firm	Date	Description and Identification
2020	Baehr & Proeschild	ca 1912	"BSW" in heart, "482", character, solid dome, sleep eyes, open mouth, for Bruno Schmidt
2023	Baehr & Proeschild	ca 1912	"BSW" in heart (with and without), "539", character, solid dome, painted eyes, closed mouth, for Bruno Schmidt
2024	Baehr & Proeschild	ca 1912	"BSW" in heart, "540", character, solid dome, painted eyes, closed mouth, for Bruno Schmidt
2025	Baehr & Proeschild	ca 1912	"BSW" in heart, "539", character, solid dome or with wig, painted eyes, closed mouth, for Bruno Schmidt
2033	Baehr & Proeschild	ca 1912	"BSW" in heart, "537", character, sleep eyes, closed mouth, for Bruno Schmidt
2042	Baehr & Proeschild	ca 1912	"BSW" in heart, character, solid dome, painted eyes, open/closed mouth
2046	Baehr & Proeschild	ca 1912	"BSW" in heart "dep", character, solid dome, painted eyes, open/closed mouth with molded tongue, for Bruno Schmidt
2048	Baehr & Proeschild	ca 1912	with and without "BSW" in heart, character, solid dome, sleep eyes, open or open/closed mouth
2050	Baehr & Proeschild	ca 1925	character, flange neck, solid dome, sleep eyes, open mouth
2069	Baehr & Proeschild	ca 1925	character, sleep eyes, closed mouth
2070	Baehr & Proeschild	ca 1920	character, baby

Mold No.	Firm	Date	Description and Identification
2072	Baehr & Proeschild	ca 1920	"BSW" with and without heart, character, sleep eyes, open or mouth, for Bruno Schmidt
2074	Baehr & Proeschild	GM 1927	character, for Bruno Schmidt, also in celluloid, new born, sleep eyes, open mouth
2075	Baehr & Proeschild	GM 1927	character, for Bruno Schmidt
2081	Baehr & Proeschild	ca 1920	character
2084	Baehr & Proeschild	ca 1920	"BP" with crossed swords, character, solid dome, sleep eyes, open mouth, for Bruno Schmidt
2085	Baehr & Proeschild	ca 1920	"BSW" in heart, character, sleep eyes, open mouth, for Bruno Schmidt
2085	Baehr & Proeschild	ca 1920	"BP" with crossed swords, otherwise as before
2092	Baehr & Proeschild	ca 1920	character, baby, for Bruno Schmidt
2094	Baehr & Proeschild	ca 1920	"BSW" in heart, character, solid dome, sleep eyes, open mouth, for Bruno Schmidt
2095	Baehr & Proeschild	ca 1920	"BSW" in heart or "BP" with crossed swords, character, solid dome or with open crown, sleep eyes, open mouth, for Bruno Schmidt
2096	Baehr & Proeschild	ca 1920	"BSW" in heart, character, solid dome, sleep eyes, open mouth, for Bruno Schmidt
2097	Baehr & Proeschild	GM 1911	"BSW" in heart, character, for Bruno Schmidt

Mold No.	Firm	Date	Description and Identification
2097	Baehr & Proeschild	GM 1911	"BP" with crossed swords, otherwise as before
2099	Baehr & Proeschild	ca 1920	"BS" in heart, "678", character, baby, for Bruno Schmidt
2144	Paul Rauschert	GM 1930	"D", character
2154	Baehr & Proeschild	ca 1920	jointed doll
2500	Schoenau & Hoffmeister	ca 1905	"SPBH", dolly face
2542	Armand Marseille	ca 1930	"AM", character, solid dome, sleep eyes, open mouth, flange neck
2542	Armand Marseille	ca 1930	"SP" in circle, Porzellanfabrik Armand Marseille (from 1948 Sonneberger Porzellanfabriken) , composition
2918	Geo. Borgfeldt & Co.	GM 1924	newborn
2966	Armand Marseille	ca 1930	"AM", character, sleep eyes, open mouth
2966	Sonneberger Porzellanfabriken	ca 1948	"SP" in circle, sleep eyes, open mouth, composition, also as black doll
3000	Armand Marseille	ca 1895	Anker with "S", shoulder head, for Philip Samhammer
3066	Armand Marseille	ca 1895	"AM", dolly face, shoulder head
3066	Sonneberger Porzellanfabriken	ca 1948	"SP" in circle, head, character, composition
3091	Armand Marseille	ca 1896	"AM", dolly face, shoulder head

Mold No.	Firm	Date	Description and Identification
3093	Armand Marseille	ca 1896	"AM", dolly face, shoulder head
3094	Armand Marseille	ca 1896	dolly face, shoulder head
3095	Armand Marseille	ca 1896	"AM", dolly face, shoulder head
3097	Armand Marseille	ca 1896	dolly face, shoulder head
3200	Armand Marseille	GM 1896	"AM", dolly face, shoulder head
3300	Armand Marseille	ca 1896	"AM", dolly face, shoulder head
3500	Armand Marseille	GM 1899	"AM", dolly face, shoulder head
3600	Armand Marseille	ca 1899	"AM DEP", dolly face
3700	Armand Marseille	ca 1899	"AM", dolly face, shoulder head
4000	Schoenau & Hoffmeister	ca 1905	"SPBH", dolly face
4001	Schoenau & Hoffmeister	ca 1905	"SPBH", dolly face
4008	Armand Marseille	ca 1900	"AM", dolly face, shoulder head
4121	Unknown	ca 1910	character, man head with cap, laughing features
4129	Nöckler & Tittel	GM 1923	"P" or "H", jointed doll, label "Schneeflöckchen"
4500	Schoenau & Hoffmeister	ca 1905	"SPBH", dolly face
4536	Paul Schmidt	ca 1923	"PS", character
4537	Paul Schmidt	ca 1923	"PS", character, sleep eyes, open mouth

Mold No.	Firm	Date	Description and Identification
4600	Schoenau & Hoffmeister	ca 1905	"SPBH", dolly face
4700	Schoenau & Hoffmeister	ca 1905	"SPBH", dolly face, shoulder head
4703	Weiss, Kühnert & Co.	ca 1913	character
4900	Schoenau & Hoffmeister	ca 1905	"SPBH", dolly face, Oriental
5000	Schoenau & Hoffmeister	GM 1903	"SPBH", dolly face
5174	Gebr. Heubach	ca 1912	character, molded hair, painted eyes, closed mouth
5300	Schoenau & Hoffmeister	ca 1905	"SPBH", dolly face
5400	Schoenau & Hoffmeister	ca 1905	"SPBH Viola", dolly face
5430	Porzellanfabrik Rauenstein	GM 1910	sulky child
5431	Porzellanfabrik Rauenstein	GM 1910	laughing face
5500	Schoenau & Hoffmeister	ca 1905	"SPBH", dolly face
5503	Gebr. Heubach	ca 1912	character, solid dome, painted googly eyes, closed mouth
5625	Gebr. Heubach	ca 1912	with sun, character, glass eyes, laughing
5630	Gebr. Heubach	ca 1915	with sun, character, sleep eyes, open mouth with tongue, 2 teeth below, laughing

Mold No.	Firm	Date	Description and Identification
5636	Gebr. Heubach	ca 1912	with sun, character, glass eyes, laughing , open/closed mouth with two molded teeth below
5689	Gebr. Heubach	ca 1912	with sun, character, glass eyes, open mouth
5700	Schoenau & Hoffmeister	ca 1905	"SPBH", dolly face
5730	Gebr. Heubach	ca 1912	with sun, character, sleep eyes, open mouth, "Santa", for Hamburger & Co
5773	Gebr. Heubach	ca 1912	character, shoulder head
5777	Gebr. Heubach	ca 1913	with sun and "Dolly Dimple", character, sleep eyes, open mouth, for Hamburger & Co.
5800	Schoenau & Hoffmeister	ca 1905	"SPBH", dolly face
6246	Gebr. Heubach	ca 1912	with square, sleep eyes, open mouth
6399	Geo. Borgfeldt & Co.	GM 1926	doll head with bobbed hair
6600	Paul Rauschert	GM 1910	"PR" with "I" or "II", character
6688	Gebr. Heubach	ca 1912	character, shoulder head, solid dome, painted eyes, closed mouth
6692	Gebr. Heubach	ca 1912	with sun, character, shoulder head, painted eyes, closed mouth, boy
6704	Gebr. Heubach	ca 1912	"Germany", character, two-face-doll, laughing, painted eyes, molded teeth, crying: painted eyes, grinning open/closed mouth

Mold No.	Firm	Date	Description and Identification
6736	Gebr. Heubach	ca 1912	with square, character, shoulder head, painted eyes, laughing, boy
6774	Gebr. Heubach	ca 1913	with square, character, painted eyes, Whistling Jim
6789	Walther & Sohn	ca 1922	"W&S", character, glass eyes, open mouth
6789	Otto Gans	ca 1922	"OG", character, sleep eyes, open mouth
6891	Gebr. Heubach	ca 1912	character, painted eyes, closed mouth
6892	Gebr. Heubach	ca 1912	with sun, character, shoulder head, painted eyes, closed mouth, boy
6894	Gebr. Heubach	ca 1912	character, painted eyes, closed mouth, boy
6896	Gebr. Heubach	ca 1912	character, painted eyes, closed mouth, boy
6897	Gebr. Heubach	ca 1912	character, painted eyes, laughing, boy
6969	Gebr. Heubach	ca 1912	with square or sun or only mold #, character, painted or glass eyes, closed mouth
6970	Gebr. Heubach	ca 1912	with sun, character, painted or glass eyes, closed mouth
6971	Gebr. Heubach	ca 1912	with sun, character, painted eyes, laughing open/closed mouth, 2 teeth below
7026	Gebr. Heubach	ca 1912	shoulder head, glass eyes, closed mouth, lady

Mold No.	Firm	Date	Description and Identification
7027	Gebr. Heubach	ca 1912	with sun, character, boy
7064	Gebr. Heubach	ca 1912	"Germany", character, solid dome with slightly molded hair, painted eyes, smiling open/closed mouth with two molded teeth, boy
7072	Gebr. Heubach	ca 1912	with sun, character, painted eyes, closed mouth, boy
7077	Gebr. Heubach	ca 1912	with sun, character with molded cap, painted eyes, closed mouth, girl
7081	Gebr. Heubach	ca 1912	character, solid dome, painted eyes, closed mouth, boy
7106	Gebr. Heubach	ca 1912	with sun, character, painted eyes, laughing, boy
7109	Gebr. Heubach	ca 1912	with sun, character, painted eyes, open/closed mouth
7124	Gebr. Heubach	ca 1912	with sun, character, shoulder head, painted eyes, open/closed mouth
7129	Gebr. Heubach	GM 1910	with sun, shoulder head, character, painted eyes, laughing, boy
7134	Gebr. Heubach	GM 1910	character, shoulder head, painted eyes, open/closed crying mouth, boy
7138	Gebr. Heubach	ca 1910	character, sleep eyes, closed mouth
7139	Gebr. Heubach	GM 1910	with square, character, shoulder head, painted eyes, open/closed mouth, girl
7144	Gebr. Heubach	ca 1910	character, painted eyes, closed mouth

Mold No.	Firm	Date	Description and Identification
7211	Gebr. Heubach	ca 1910	with square, character, painted eyes, open/closed laughing mouth
7226	Gebr. Heubach	ca 1910	with square, character, molded cap, painted eyes, closed mouth, girl
7246	Gebr. Heubach	ca 1912	with sun or square, character, sleep eyes, closed mouth
7247	Gebr. Heubach	ca 1912	with sun, character, glass eyes, closed mouth
7248	Gebr. Heubach	ca 1912	with sun, character, glass eyes, closed mouth
7256	Gebr. Heubach	ca 1912	character, glass eyes, closed mouth
7307	Gebr. Heubach	ca 1912	character, painted eyes, laughing open/closed mouth with molded teeth
7314	Gebr. Heubach	ca 1912	with square, character, painted eyes, laughing
7326	Gebr. Heubach	ca 1912	shoulder head, type lady
7345	Gebr. Heubach	ca 1912	with sun or square, character, shoulder head, painted eyes, smiling, boy
7346	Gebr. Heubach	ca 1912	with sun or square, character, shoulder head, glass eyes, closed mouth
7377	Unknown	ca 1915	"made in Germany", Kewpie flange neck, googly eyes, closed laughing mouth
7402	Gebr. Heubach	ca 1912	character, painted eyes, laughing
7407	Gebr. Heubach	ca 1912	character, glass eyes, closed mouth

Mold No.	Firm	Date	Description and Identification
7448	Gebr. Heubach	ca 1912	character, painted little eyes, grinning open/closed mouth, crying
7550	Gebr. Heubach	ca 1912	character, sleep eyes, open/closed mouth with molded tongue
7587	Gebr. Heubach	ca 1914	with square, character, painted googly eyes, closed mouth
7602	Gebr. Heubach	ca 1912	with sun or square, character, painted eyes, closed mouth (ca 1930 also in composition)
7603	Gebr. Heubach	ca 1912	with sun, character, solid dome, painted or glass eyes, closed mouth
7604	Gebr. Heubach	ca 1912	with sun or square, character, painted eyes, laughing , open/closed mouth with 2 teeth below, or with glass eyes and wig, boy
7612	Gebr. Heubach	ca 1912	with sun, character, solid dome, painted hair, painted eyes, closed mouth
7614	Gebr. Heubach	ca 1912	with square, character, painted eyes, boy
7616	Gebr. Heubach	ca 1912	character, shoulder head, glass eyes, open/closed mouth
7620	Gebr. Heubach	ca 1912	with square or sun, character, painted eyes, open/closed mouth with two painted teeth, also as black doll, boy
7622	Gebr. Heubach	ca 1912	with sun, character, painted eyes, closed mouth, boy

Mold No.	Firm	Date	Description and Identification
7623	Gebr. Heubach	ca 1912	with sun, character, painted eyes, open/closed mouth
7624	Gebr. Heubach	GM 1910	character
7625	Gebr. Heubach	GM 1910	character
7631	Gebr. Heubach	ca 1912	character, painted eyes, closed mouth, boy
7634	Gebr. Heubach	ca 1912	with sun, character, painted eyes, crying grinning mouth, boy
7663 5	Gebr. Heubach	GM 1910	character
7636	Gebr. Heubach	GM 1910	character
7637	Gebr. Heubach	ca 1912	with sun, character, painted eyes, smiling
7644	Gebr. Heubach	GM 1910	with sun or square, character, shoulder head, painted eyes, laughing, boy
7647	Gebr. Heubach	ca 1912	with sun, character, painted eyes, open/closed laughing mouth
7650	Gebr. Heubach	ca 1912	character, glass eyes, open/closed mouth
7654	Gebr. Heubach	ca 1912	character, shoulder head, painted eyes, open/closed mouth with 2 molded teeth
7657	Gebr. Heubach	GM 1910	character
7658	Gebr. Heubach	GM 1910	character, shoulder head, molded hair, painted eyes, open/closed mouth, black doll

Mold No.	Firm	Date	Description and Identification
7659	Gebr. Heubach	GM 1910	character
7661	Gebr. Heubach	ca 1912	with sun, character with molded black dollhair, painted eyes, laughing open/closed mouth
7665	Gebr. Heubach	ca 1912	with sun, character, sleep eyes, open/closed mouth, 2 teeth upper, smiling
7668	Gebr. Heubach	ca 1912	with sun, character, molded hair, painted eyes, open/closed mouth, black doll
7669	Gebr. Heubach	ca 1912	with sun, character, glass eyes, open/closed mouth, often on mechanism walking doll
7670	Gebr. Heubach	ca 1912	with sun, character, black doll
7671	Gebr. Heubach	ca 1912	with sun, character, black doll
7672	Gebr. Heubach	ca 1912	"Germany", character, molded hair, painted Intaglio eyes, closed mouth
7679	Gebr. Heubach	ca 1912	character, glass eyes, open/closed mouth
7682	Gebr. Heubach	ca 1912	with square, character, sleep eyes, open mouth
7684	Gebr. Heubach	ca 1912	with sun, character, solid dome, painted eyes, open/closed crying mouth
7686	Gebr. Heubach	GM 1911	character, glass eyes, open/closed mouth with molded tongue
7687	Gebr. Heubach	GM 1911	character

Mold No.	Firm	Date	Description and Identification
7692	Gebr. Heubach	GM 1911	character
7701	Gebr. Heubach	GM 1911	character
7703	Gebr. Heubach	ca 1911	with sun, character, molded hair with bow, painted eyes, laughing
7711	Gebr. Heubach	ca 1912	with sun or square, character, glass eyes, open mouth
7714	Gebr. Heubach	GM 1911	character
7739	Gebr. Heubach	GM 1911	character
7740	Gebr. Heubach	GM 1911	character
7743	Gebr. Heubach	ca 1912	with sun, character, painted eyes, smiling, open/closed mouth, boy
7744	Gebr. Heubach	ca 1912	with sun, character, painted eyes, pouty mouth, boy
7745	Gebr. Heubach	ca 1912	with sun, character, painted eyes, laughing open/closed mouth with 2 teeth, boy
7759	Gebr. Heubach	ca 1912	with sun or square, character, painted eyes, closed mouth, boy
7760	Gebr. Heubach	ca 1912	with sun, character, painted eyes, closed mouth, boy
7761	Gebr. Heubach	ca 1912	with sun, character, painted eyes, open/closed mouth, crying (same as shoulder head mold # 7843)
7763	Gebr. Heubach	ca 1912	with sun or square, character, molded hair with bow, painted eyes, closed mouth, girl

Mold No.	Firm	Date	Description and Identification
7764	Gebr. Heubach	ca 1912	with square, character, molded hair with bow, painted eyes, open/closed mouth, singing, girl
7768	Gebr. Heubach	ca 1912	with square, molded hair with bow, character, painted eyes, closed mouth, girl
7779	Gebr. Heubach	ca 1912	with sun, character, molded cap, painted
7781	Gebr. Heubach	ca 1912	with sun, character, solid dome, painted eyes, open/closed crying mouth
7788	Gebr. Heubach	ca 1912	with square, character, molded hair with bow
7843	Gebr. Heubach	ca 1912	with square, shoulder head, (same as mold # 7761)
7850	Gebr. Heubach	ca 1912	with square, character, shoulder head, molded hair with bow, painted eyes, closed smiling mouth with molded teeth, girl
7851	Gebr. Heubach	ca 1912	with square, character, (same as mold # 7850)
7852	Gebr. Heubach	ca 1912	with square, character, molded hair, painted eyes, open/closed smiling mouth with molded teeth
7859	Gebr. Heubach	ca 1912	with square, shoulder head, character, molded hair with bow, painted eyes, closed mouth
7864	Gebr. Heubach	ca 1912	character, shoulder head, glass eyes, closed mouth

Mold No.	Firm	Date	Description and Identification
7867	Gebr. Heubach	ca 1912	with square, character, shoulder head, molded hair, painted eyes, closed mouth, girl
7867	Gebr. Heubach	ca 1912	with head, otherwise as before
7885	Gebr. Heubach	ca 1912	with square, character, molded hair, bow painted eyes, closed mouth
7890	Gebr. Heubach	ca 1912	character, molded hair, bow, painted eyes, girl
7911	Gebr. Heubach	ca 1912	with square, character, painted eyes, laughing open/closed mouth, boy
7925	Gebr. Heubach	ca 1914	character, shoulder head, glass eyes, smiling, open mouth, lady
7926	Gebr. Heubach	ca 1912	character, shoulder head, glass eyes, smiling, open mouth, lady
7956	Gebr. Heubach	ca 1912	with square, character, molded hair, painted eyes, closed mouth, girl
7959	Gebr. Heubach	ca 1912	with square, character, molded cap, painted eyes, open/closed mouth
7971	Gebr. Heubach	ca 1912	character, painted eyes, laughing, boy
7975	Gebr. Heubach	ca 1912	with sun or square, molded, take off bonnet, made of bisque with roses or pink colored or yellow ribbon, sleep eyes, closed mouth
7977	Gebr. Heubach	ca 1912	with sun or square, character, molded cap with painted different flowers, painted eyes, closed mouth
7917	Gebr. Heubach	ca 1914	with sun, character, sleep eyes, closed mouth

Mold No.	Firm	Date	Description and Identification
7996	Gebr. Heubach	ca 1914	with sun, character, glass eyes, closed mouth
8017	Gebr. Heubach	ca 1912	"Germany", character, glass eyes, closed mouth
8035	Gebr. Heubach	ca 1912	with square, character, solid dome, painted eyes, closed mouth, boy
8050	Gebr. Heubach	ca 1912	character, molded plaited hair with blue hair ribbon, painted eyes, laughing, girl
8055	Gebr. Heubach	ca 1912	with square, character, shoulder head, painted eyes, laughing , closed mouth
8170	Kämmer & Reinhardt	GM 1925	see K&R mold # 170
8171	Kämmer & Reinhardt	GM 1925	see K&R mold # 171
8172	Kämmer & Reinhardt	GM 1925	see K&R mold # 172
8173	Kämmer & Reinhardt	GM 1925	see K&R mold # 173
8175	Kämmer & Reinhardt	GM 1928	see K&R mold # 175
8178	Gebr. Heubach	GM1911	with sun and "DRGM 486 986 Germany", character, molded and painted eyes, open/closed mouth, (DRGM = Franz Belouschek)
8191	Gebr. Heubach	ca 1912	with square, character, painted eyes, laughing, boy
8192	Gebr. Heubach	ca 1914	with sun or square, character, sleep eyes, open mouth

Mold No.	Firm	Date	Description and Identification
8195	Gebr. Heubach	ca 1912	with square, character, shoulder head, painted eyes, closed mouth, boy
8202	Gebr. Heubach	ca 1912	with square, character, molded hair with bounded hair and bow in front, painted googly eyes, closed mouth
8204	Gebr. Heubach	ca 1912	with sun, character, sleep eyes, closed mouth
8226	Gebr. Heubach	ca 1912	with square, character, shoulder head, molded cap, painted eyes, closed mouth, girl
8232	Gebr. Heubach	ca 1914	character, shoulder head, glass eyes, open mouth
8306	Gebr. Heubach	ca 1912	with square, character, shoulder head, solid dome with molded hair, painted eyes, laughing open/closed mouth with molded teeth, boy
8309	Gebr. Heubach	ca 1912	with square, character, painted eyes, laughing, boy
8316	Gebr. Heubach	ca 1912	with square, character, sleep eyes, open/closed laughing mouth with molded teeth
8358	Gebr. Heubach	ca 1912	with square, character, molded bobbed hair
8381	Gebr. Heubach	ca 1911	with square, character, molded hair, plaited hair over head, painted eyes, closed mouth (presumably Princess Juliane of Netherland)
8407	Gebr. Heubach	ca 1912	with square, character, glass eyes, closed mouth

Mold No.	Firm	Date	Description and Identification
8413	Gebr. Heubach	ca 1914	with square, character, sleep eyes, open/closed mouth
8316	Gebr. Heubach	ca 1914	with square, character, glass eyes, laughing
8420	Gebr. Heubach	ca 1914	with square, character, sleep eyes, open or closed mouth
8457	Gebr. Heubach	ca 1913	with square, character, shoulder head, Indian
8459	Gebr. Heubach	ca 1914	character, sleep eyes, laughing
8473	Gebr. Heubach	ca 1914	with square, character, glass eyes, open/closed mouth
8480	Gebr. Heubach	ca 1912	with square, character, sleep eyes, closed mouth
8547	Gebr. Heubach	ca 1912	with square, character, shoulder head, painted eyes, closed mouth, girl
8548	Gebr. Heubach	ca 1912	with square, character, painted or glass eyes, closed pouty mouth
8552	Limbach AG.	ca 1911	with clover-leaf, shoulder head, type lady, with molded hair and ribbon, painted eyes, open/closed mouth with molded teeth, molded blouse
8553	Limbach AG.	ca 1911	with clover-leaf, shoulder head, type lady, with molded hair and ribbon
8555	Gebr. Heubach	ca 1912	with square, solid dome, painted googly eyes, closed mouth, boy

Mold No.	Firm	Date	Description and Identification
8556	Gebr. Heubach	ca 1912	with square, solid dome, painted eyes, littler open/closed mouth
8572	Gebr. Heubach	ca 1912	character, painted eyes,
8588	Gebr. Heubach	ca 1912	with square, character, painted eyes, closed pouty mouth
8589	Gebr. Heubach	ca 1914	with square, character, painted googly eyes, closed mouth
8590	Gebr. Heubach	ca 1914	character, solid dome, painted googly eyes, closed mouth, boy
8606	Gebr. Heubach	ca 1914	character, painted googly eyes, closed mouth
8661	Gebr. Heubach	ca 1914	character, solid dome, painted eyes, closed mouth
8668	Gebr. Heubach	ca 1914	character, solid dome, glass eyes, closed mouth
8678	Gebr. Heubach	ca 1914	with square, character, googly eyes, closed smiling mouth
8682	Limbach AG.	ca 1911	with clover-leaf, character, molded hair, painted or glass eyes, open/closed mouth
8723	Gebr. Heubach	ca 1912	with sun, "EINCO", character, big googly eyes with lever for eye-moving, closed mouth, for Eisenmann & Co.
8724	Gebr. Heubach	ca 1914	character, shoulder head, painted eyes, open/closed smiling mouth
8729	Gebr. Heubach	ca 1914	with square, character, painted googly eyes, open/closed mouth

Mold No.	Firm	Date	Description and Identification
8759	Gebr. Heubach	ca 1914	with square, character, molded babycap, painted eyes, open/closed mouth with molded tongue
8764	Gebr. Heubach	ca 1914	"EINCO", character, shoulder head, googly eyes, closed mouth, for Eisenmann & Co.
8774	Gebr. Heubach	ca 1914	with sun or square, character, painted eyes, Whistling Jim
8778	Gebr. Heubach	GM 1913	Grandma
8801	Gebr. Heubach	ca 1914	character, shoulder head, painted eyes, laughing
8806	Gebr. Heubach	ca 1914	with square, shoulder head, character, solid dome, painted eyes, open laughing mouth with molded teeth and molded tongue, boy
8836	Gebr. Heubach	ca 1914	with sun, character, glass eyes, open/closed mouth with small hole, molded tongue, 2 teeth below
8867	Limbach AG.	ca 1926	newborn, for Louis Amberg & Son
8878	Gebr. Heubach	ca 1914	with square, character, painted eyes, laughing, boy
9042	Gebr. Heubach	ca 1914	character, shoulder head
9056	Gebr. Heubach	ca 1914	with square, character, painted googly eyes, closed mouth
9072	Gebr. Heubach	ca 1914	character, painted eyes, closed mouth, boy
9081	Gebr. Heubach	ca 1914	character, painted googly eyes, closed mouth

Mold No.	Firm	Date	Description and Identification
9085	Gebr. Heubach	ca 1914	with square, character, solid dome with a small hole for a pig tail, painted googly eyes, closed mouth
9100	Gebr. Heubach	ca 1914	with square, laughing cat head with painted eyes
9141	Gebr. Heubach	ca 1914	with square, character, right painted googly eye, left eye twinkle, closed mouth
9145	Gebr. Heubach	ca 1914	character, solid dome, painted eyes, closed mouth
9167	Gebr. Heubach	ca 1914	with square, character, painted eyes, closed mouth
9209	Gebr. Heubach	ca 1914	with square, clownshead
9219	Gebr. Heubach	ca 1914	character, painted eyes, closed mouth
9355	Gebr. Heubach	ca 1914	with square, character, shoulder head, sleep eyes, open mouth
9457	Gebr. Heubach	ca 1914	with square, character, expressive face, old man as Eskimo or Indian
9268	Unknown	ca 1912	Kewpie-shoulder head
9335	Gebr. Heubach	ca 1914	with square, character, shoulder head, painted eyes, open/closed mouth, black doll
9500	Rudolph Heinz & Co.	ca 1922	"AV Neuhaus am Rwg.", dolly face
9501	Rudolph Heinz & Co.	ca 1922	"Neuhaus am Rwg.", dolly face
9513	Gebr. Heubach	ca 1914	with square, character, googly eyes, closed mouth

Mold No.	Firm	Date	Description and Identification
9570	Gebr. Heubach	ca 1914	character, solid dome, molded hair, painted eyes, open/closed mouth
9572	Gebr. Heubach	ca 1914	with square, character, googly eyes, closed mouth
9573	Gebr. Heubach	ca 1914	with square, character, googly eyes, closed mouth
9578	Gebr. Heubach	ca 1914	with square, character, googly eyes, closed mouth
9594	Gebr. Heubach	ca 1914	with square, character, painted googly eyes, closed mouth
10532	Gebr. Heubach	**ca 1920**	with square, character, sleep eyes, open mouth
10539	Gebr. Heubach	ca 1920	with square, character, sleep eyes, open mouth, for Wagner & Zetsche
10542	Gebr. Heubach	ca 1920	with square, character, googly sleep eyes, closed mouth
10556	Gebr. Heubach	ca 1920	with square, shoulder head, character, (see mold # 10539 - see mold # 200)
10557	Gebr. Heubach	ca 1920	with square, character, (same as mold # 10539)
10566	Gebr. Heubach	ca 1920	see mold # 10539 for Wagner & Zetsche
10586	Gebr. Heubach	ca 1920	with square with and without "W.Z.I.", character, (same as mold # 10539), for Wagner & Zetsche, Ilmenau
10588	Gebr. Heubach	ca 1920	with square, character, (same as mold # 10539)

The following letters were found as abbreviations on doll heads, also a few on doll bodies. These markings are either marks, trademarks or labels of doll factories, porcelain manufactories or import houses.

Letter	Firm
A	
ABG	Alt, Beck & Gottschalck, Nauendorf
AF&C	Fleischmann & Creamer, Sonneberg
AH	Adolf Heller, Waltershausen
AHS	Albin Hess, Schalkau
AHW	Adolf Heller, Waltershausen
AHE	Adolf Hülss, Waltershausen
AK	A. Kröhl, Berlin
ALB	Adolf Landsberger, Magdeburg
ALS	Anton Link, Saulgau
AM	Armand
AM	A. Michaelis, Rauenstein
AeM	A.C. Anger, Böhmen
AMN	Andreas Müller, Sonneberg
AP	Adolf Prouza, Böhmen
AR	Theodor Recknagel, Alexandrinenthal

Letter	Firm
AR	August Riedeler, Königsee
AS	Arthur Schoenau, Sonneberg
AS	August Steiner, Köppelsdorf
AV	Porzellanfabrik Neuhaus am Rennsteig
AW	Adolf Wislizenus, Waltershausen
AWW	Adolf Wislizenus, Waltershausen

B

BJ&Co	B. Illfelder & Co., Fürth
BP	Baehr & Proeschild, Ohrdruf
BP	Buchauer Porzellanfabrik Plass & Roesner
BP	Swaine & Co, Hüttensteinach
B&P	Beahr & Proeschild, Ohrdruf
BS	Bruno Schmidt, Waltershausen
BSW	Bruno Schmidt, Waltershausen

C

C	Casseler Puppenfabrik M.R. Rosenstein jr.
C	Cuno & Otto Dressel, Sonneberg
C	Dressel & Koch, Köppelsdorf
CB	Carl Bergmann, Sonneberg
CC	Unbekannt
CEGD	C. Erich Günther, Dresden
CE&S	Christian Eichhorn & Söhne, Steinach
CEUS	Christian Eichhorn & Söhne, Steinach
CF&Co	Carl Feiler & Co., Jena
CH	Christian Hopf, Neustadt
CH	Carl Hartmann, Neustadt
CHND	Carl Horn Nachf., Dresden
CK	Carl Knoll, Böhmen
CKF	Carl Krahmer, Frankenhausen
COD	Cuno & Otto Dressel, Sonneberg
CP	Catterfelder Puppenfabrik, Catterfeld
CPMRRjr	Casseler Puppenfabrik M.R. Rosenstein jr.
C&S	Curnen & Steiner, Sonneberg
CT	Carl Trautmann, Finsterbergen
CV	Closter Veilsdorf

Letter	Firm
D	
D	Julius Dorst, Sonneberg
D	Cuno & Otto Dressel, Sonneberg
D I	Swaine & Co., Hüttensteinach
DEP	= deponiert, - DEP
DGMSch	=Deutscher Gebrauchs-Muster-Schutz
DIP	Swaine & Co., Hüttensteinach
D&K	Dressel & Koch, Köppelsdorf
DKF	Dornheim, Koch & Fischer, Gräfenroda
D&PC	Dressel & Pietschmann, Coburg
D.P.	Hamburger & Co., Berlin
DP	Dora Petzold, Berlin
DRGM	= Deutsches Reichs-Gebrauchs-Muster
DRMR	=Deutsche Reichs-Muster-Rolle
DRP	=Deutsches Reichs-Patent
DV	Swaine & Co., Hüttensteinach
E	
EBVR	Emil Bauersachs, Sonneberg
ED	E. Dehler, Coburg
ED	Cuno & Otto Dressel, Sonneberg
EDH	E. Dehler, Coburg
EG	Edgard Goldstein & Co., Berlin
EG	Ernst Gromann, Sonneberg
EH	Ernst Heubach, Köppelsdorf
EHK	Ernst Heubach, Köppelsdorf
EK	Ernst Klötzer, Sonneberg
EK	Edmund Knoch, Mönchröden
EL	Ernst Liebermann, Neustadt
EM	Ernst Metzler, Pressig-Rothenkirchen
EP	Ernst Pfeiffer, Wien
E&S	Christian Eichhorn & Söhne, Steinach
ESTP	Erste Steinbacher Porzellanfabrik, Steinbach
EUST	Edmund Ulrich Steiner, Sonneberg
EvB	Erich von Berg, Steinach

Letter	Firm
EW	Ernst Winkler, Sonneberg
EWH	Ernst Wehncke, Hamburg
EZ	Emil Zitzmann, Steinach

F

FB	Fritz Bierschenk, Sonneberg
F&B	Fleischmann & Bloedel, Fürth
F&BF	Fleischmann & Bloedel, Fürth
FEWB	Friedr. Edm. Winkler, Sonneberg
FNC	Fischer, Naumann & Co., Ilmenau
FNI	Fischer, Naumann & Co., Ilmenau
FN&Co	Fischer, Naumann & Co., Ilmenau
FP	Friedrichsrodaer Puppenfabrik
FS	Franz Schmidt & Co., Georgenthal
FS&Co	Franz Schmidt & Co., Georgenthal
FWB	F. Welsch, Breslau

G

G	Georg Gebert, Berlin
GB	Geo. Borgfeldt & Co., Berlin
GbrK	Gebr. Kühnlenz, Kronach
G&Co	Greiner & Co., Steinach
GDF	Unbekannt
GH	Gustav Heubach, Steinbach
GH	Gebr. Heubach, Lichte
GK	Gebr. Kühnlenz, Kronach
GKN	Gebr. Knoch, Neustadt
GL	Georg Lutz, Sonneberg
GL	Unbekannt
GM	=Geschmacks-Muster-Schutz
GMS	=Gebrauchs-Muster-Schutz
GS	Gans & Seyfarth, Waltershausen
GS	Gebr. Süssenguth, Neustadt
G&S	Gutmann & Schiffnie, Nürnberg
G&S	Gans & Seyfarth, Waltershausen
GT	Gerber & Tesuch, Sonneberg
GW	Gustav Wohlleben, Neustadt

Letter	Firm

H

H	Heinrich Handwerck, Waltershausen
HC	Heber & Co., Neustadt
HcHH	Heinrich Handwerck, Waltershausen
H&Co.	Hamburger & Co., Nürnberg
HH	Hermann Heyde, Dresden
HH	Heinrich Handwerck, Waltershausen
HHD	Hermann Heyde, Dresden
HHW	Heinrich Handwerck, Waltershausen
HJL	H.J. Leven, Sonneberg
HL	Unbekannt
HPF	Herzpuppenfabrik, Berlin
HS	Hermann Steiner, Neustadt
HSN	Hermann Steiner, Neustadt
HSt	Hermann Steiner, Neustadt
HW	Heinrich Handwerck, Waltershausen
HWENSPF	Hermann Wolf, Nordhausen
HWN	Hugo Wiegand, Waltershausen

I

IB	Iris Beaumont, Berlin

J

JDK	J.D. Kestner jr., Waltershausen
JDS	Julius Dorst, Sonneberg
JH&S	Julius Hering & Sohn, Köppelsdorf
JIO	Alt, Beck & Gottschalck, Neuendorf
JK	Theodor Recknagel, Alexandrinenthal
JMS	Julia Müller-Sarne, Dresden

K

KB	Unbekannt
K&Co	Kestner & Comp., Ohrdruf
KH	Karl Hartmann, Stockheim
K&H	Kley & Hahn, Ohrdruf
KK	Käthe Kruse, Bad Kösen

Letter	Firm
KPM	Königl. Porzellanmanufaktur Meissen
KPM	Königl. Porzellanmanufaktur Berlin
KPM	A.W.Fr. Kistner, Scheibe
KPN	Karl Pietsch, Oeslau
KR	Kämmer & Reinhardt, Waltershausen
K&R	Kämmer & Reinhardt, Waltershausen
KW	Kohl & Wengenroth, Offenbach
K&W	Koch & Weithase, Köppelsdorf

L

LA&S	Louis Amberg & Son, Sonneberg
LD	Löffler & Dill, Sonneberg
L&D	Löffler & Dill, Sonneberg
L&DS	Löffler & Dill, Sonneberg
L&H	Leibe & Hofmann, Gera-Untermhaus
LHB	Unbekannt
*LHK	Unbekannt
LL&S	Louis Lindner & Söhne, Sonneberg
L&M	Unbekannt
LPL	Louis Philipp Luthardt, Neustadt
LRS	Louis Roth, Sonneberg
LS	Lambert & Samhammer, Sonneberg
LW&C	Louis Wolf & Co., Sonneberg

M

M	Unbekannt
M	Ma.E. Maar, Mönchröden
MB	Arthur Schoenau, Sonneberg
MCo	Karl Müller & Co., Effelder
MH	Unbekannt
MKW	Josef Strasser, München
MMM	Ma.E. Maar, Mönchröden
MOA	Max Oscar Arnold, Neustadt
MR	Moritz Resek, Böhmen
MRW	Max Rudolph, Waltershausen
M&S	Müller & Strasburger, Sonneberg

Letter	Firm
MSS	Mylius Sperschneider, Sonneberg

N

NG	=Neugeborenes, Geradhals (Theodor Recknagel Alexandrinenthal)
NK	=Neugeborenes, Kurbelkopf (Theodor Recknagel, Alexandrinenthal)
NT	Nöckler & Tittel, Schneeberg
N&T	Nöckler & Tittel, Schneeberg

O

OB	Oskar Büchner, Ebersdorf
OCo	H. Offenbacher & Co., Nürnberg
OG	Otto Gans, Waltershausen
OIC	J.D. Kestner jr., Waltershausen
OS	Otto Schamberger, Sonneberg
OWN	Otto Wohlmann, Nürnberg

P

PH	Paul Hunaeus, Hannover
P&H	Pollak & Hoffmann, Böhmen
PM	Porzellanfabrik Mengersgereuth
PN	S. Bergmann jr. & Co.
PN	Porzellanfabrik Neuhaus
PR	Paul Rauschert, Pressig
PR	Hermann Rösel, Nürnberg
P&R	Plass & Roesner, Böhmen
PS	Paul Schmidt, Sonneberg
PSch	Paul Scherf, Sonneberg
PSSth	Paul Schmidt, Sonneberg
PZ	Paul Zierow, Berlin

R

R	Theodor Recknagel, Alexandrinenthal
RA	Theodor Recknagel, Alexandrinenthal

Letter	Firm
RB	Rempel & Breitung, Sonneberg
RBW	Richard Beck & Co., Waltershausen
RC	Robert Carl, Köppelsdorf
RDEP	Max Räder, Sonneberg
RL	Rudolf Leschhorn, Sonneberg
Rn	Porzellanfabrik Rauenstein
R&SS	Rauch & Schelhorn, Sonneberg
RBW	Richard Beck & Co., Waltershausen

S

S	Theodor Recknagel, Alexandrinenthal
S&C	Swaine & Co., Hüttensteinach (gestempelt)
S&C	Franz Schmidt & Co., Georgenthal
SH	Simon & Halbirg, Gräfenhain
S&H	Simon & Halbirg, Gräfenhain
SMB	Sigismund Markmann, Berlin
S&M	Seligmann & Mayer, Sonneberg
SP	Sonneberger Porzellanfabrik
SPBH	Schoenau & Hoffmeister, Porzellanfabrik Burggrub
SPS	vermutlich Sonneberger Porzellanfabrik, Carl Müller, Sonneberg
SQ	Schützmeister & Quendt, Boilstädt
SS	M.F. Schelhorn, Sonneberg
SSN	S. Schwerin Nachf., Breslau
SUN	Sigismund Ullmann, Nürnberg
SUR	Seyfarth & Reinhardt, Waltershausen
SW	Strobel & Wilken, Sonneberg
S&W	Strobel & Wilken, Sonneberg
SWC	Unbekannt

T

TH	Theodor Hörnlein, Sonneberg
TKB	M. Tersch, Berlin
TP	Theodor Pohl, Böhmen
TPI	Thüringer Puppenindustrie, Waltershausen
TPIW	Thüringer Puppenindustrie, Waltershausen
TR	Unbekannt

Letter	Firm
TW	Theodor Wendt, Hamburg
V	
VMB	Valentin Moritz Bruchlos, Eisfeld
W	
W	Albert Wacker, Bayerische Celluloidwarenfabrik, Nürnberg
W	Heubach, Kämpfe & Sontag, Wallendorf
W	E. Winkler, Sonneberg
W&Co.	Wiefel & Co., Steinbach
WD	Unbekannt
WEP	Wenzel Prouza, Böhmen
WEV	Unbekannt
WG	F&W Goebel, Oeslau
WK	Werner Krauth, Leipzig
WSK	Wiesenthal, Schindel & Kallenberg, Waltershausen
SKS	Strasser & Co., München
WP	Waltershäuser Puppenfabrik, Waltershausen
W&S	Walther & Sohn, Oeslau
WSt	Wilhelm Strunz, Nürnberg
WsT	Weiskirchlitzer Steingutfabrik, Böhmen
WUZI	Wagner & Zetsche, Ilmenau
WZ	Wagner & Zetsche, Ilmenau
WZI	Wagner & Zetsche, Ilmenau
Z	
Z	Gottlieb Zinner & Söhne, Schalkau

1

The names and terms listed in the following are either registered trademarks or word used by porecelain manufactories, doll factories or import houses. They were found as marks or labels or printed on the packing. The registered terms of Rheinische Gummi- and Celluloidfabrik of Mannheim-Neckarau (turtle-mark) are not considered here. This would go beyond the frame of this publication, and is the subject of another report by the authors. Comparing registered trademarks with foreign doll litereature may lead to some misunderstandings. United States import houses had the same trademarks registered as their own trademarks at different points of time. The first registration had often been made with the German authorities (or vice versa), thus two different dates of registration could exist. The dates mentioned in this publication refer exclusively to the year of registration in Germany.

Mark- or article	=	Applied or used by the firm

A

ABC-Puppen	-	Butler Brothers, Sonneberg
Adeline	1927	E. Liebermann, Neustadt
Adlon	1922	O. Schamberger, Sonneberg
Admiral Dewey and his man	-	Cuno & Otto Dressel, Sonneberg
Agnes	-	Butler Brothers, Sonneberg
Aha-Puppe	1925	Andreas Hofmann, Fürth
AHABE	1925	Amberg & Hergershausen, Berlin

Mark- or article	=	Applied or used by the firm
Al-Al	1923	Arno Lützelberger, Ilmenau
Alah	1924	Anni Lonz, Koblenz
Albego	-	Alt, Beck & Gottschalck, Nauendorf
Alice	-	Porzellanfabrik Rauenstein
Alkico	-	A. Kiesewetter, Coburg
All Nation Comical	-	Cuno & Otto Dressel, Sonneberg
Alm	1900	Gebr. Borgfeldt & Co., Berlin
Alma	1901	Armand Marseille, Köppelsdorf
American Beauty	-	Robert Carl, Köppelsdorf
American Pet	-	F.M. Schilling, Sonneberg
American Queen	1905	Otto Morgenroth, Sonneberg
Ameli	-	Kämmer & Reinhardt, Waltershausen
A mon Mignon	1895	Fleischmann & Bloedel, Nürnberg
Amuso	1925	A. Möller & Sohn, Georgenthal
Anna	1891	Schwarzkopf & Fröber, Sonneberg
Apriko	1921	Margarete Steiff, Giengen/Albert Schlopsnies, München
ARI	-	A. Riedeler, Königsee
Arnola	1914	Max Oscar Arnold, Neustadt
Arnoldia	1910	Sing- und Sprechpuppen AG., Neustadt
Asador	1926	Bauer & Richter, Stadtroda
Asta	1927	Arthur Schoenau, Sonneberg
As You like	1904	Buschow & Beck, Nossen
Autoliebchen	1912	Arthur Schoenau, Sonneberg

B

Baby	1911	Hermann Kröning, Gotha
Baby Bauz	1910	Kämmer & Reinhardt, Waltershausen
Baby Bauz	1910	Käthe Kruse Werkstätten, Bad Kösen
Baby Belle	1908	C.M. Bergmann, Waltershausen
Baby Belle	1908	Geo. Borgfeldt & Co., Berlin
Baby Betty	1912	Armand Marseille, Köppelsdorf
Baby Betty	1912	Butler Brothers GmbH., Sonneberg
Baby Blanche	-	Simon & Halbig, Gräfenhain
Baby Bo-Kaye	1926	Geo. Borgfeldt & Co., Berlin
Baby Bunting	1884	Louis Lindner & Söhne, Sonneberg
Baby Bud	1915	Butler Brothers, Sonneberg

Mark- or article	=	Applied or used by the firm
Baby Cut	1914	Heinrich Handwerck, Waltershausen
Baby Joan	1927	Ernst Liebermann, Neustadt
Baby Gloria	1920	Armand Marseille, Köppelsdorf
Baby Phyllis	1925	Armand Marseille, Köppelsdorf
Baby Smiles	1926	Geo. Borgfeldt & Co., Berlin
Baby Tufams	-	Louis Amberg & Son, Sonneberg
Bärbel-Puppe	1922	Bärbel Wichmann, Berlin
Backfischpuppen	-	Cuno & Otto Dressel, Sonneberg
Baigneur habille	-	Wilhelm Simon & Co., Hildburghausen
Bambina	1909	Cuno & Otto Dressel, Sonneberg
Beauty	1898	Armand Marseille, Köppelsdorf
Beauty	1898	W.A. Cissna & Co., Chicago (USA)
Bebe Articule	1899	Emil Pfeiffer, Wien
Bebe Articule	1899	F.E. Winkler, Sonneberg
Bebe Carmencita	1920	Arthur Schoenau, Sonneberg
Bebe Coiffeure	1911	Gutmann & Schiffnie, Sonneberg
Bebe Cosmopolite	1895	Heinrich Handwerk, Waltershausen
Bebe Elite	1901	Max Handwerck, Waltershausen
Bebe Habille	1900	Carl Geyer, Sonneberg
Bebe l'Avenir	1907	Gutmann & Schiffnie, Sonneberg
Bebe l'Avenir	1907	Gebr. Süssenguth, Neustadt
Bebe Kochniss	-	Carl Kochniss, Sonneberg
Bebe Princess	1921	Gebr. Ohlhaver, Sonneber
Bebe Reclame	1898	Heinrich Handwerck, Waltershausen
Bebe Superior	1913	Heinrich Handwerck, Waltershausen
Bebe tout en bois	1914	E. Dehler, Neustadt
Bebe tout en bois	1914	Rudolf Schneider, Sonneberg
Bebe Triomphe	1898	Fleischmann & Bloedel, Nürnberg
Beha	1927	Berthold Helk, Neustadt
Bella	1924	Leo Nordschild, Berlin
Bellamit	1923	A.M. Jochachimsczyk, Berlin
Bertha	-	Butler Brothers, Sonneberg
Bepi-Puppen	1925	Bergische Puppenindustrie, Remscheid
Betsy	1923	Geo. Borgfeld & Co., Berlin
Bette	1893	J. D. Kestner jr., Waltershausen
Bi-Ba-Bo	1908	Julius Jeidel, Frankfurt
Bi, Ba, Bo	1927	Weise & Co., Leipzig
Biddy Baby	-	M. Kohnstamm & Co., Fürth
Billydoll	1909	Margarete Steiff, Giengen

Mark- or article	=	Applied or used by the firm
Bisculoid	1929	Hertwig & Co., Katzhütte
Biskuit Imitation	1886	A. Zeh, Sonneberg
Biskuit Imitation	1886	Gebr. Haag, Sonneberg
Bisquitfacon	1878	Barbara Schilling, Sonneberg
Bonnie Babe	1926	Geo. Borgfeldt & Co., Berlin
Brüderchen	1929	Friedrichsrodaer Puppenfabrik
Boy Scouts	1914	Gutmann & Schiffnie, Sonneberg
Bubikopf	1925	S. Plaut, Düsseldorf
Bufli	1924	Resi Brandl, Berlin
Buporit	1909	Baehr & Proeschild, Ohrdruf
Bussi	-	Willi Steiner, Freiburg
Bussi	-	Eugen Knops, Freiburg
Butler	-	Unbekannt
Butzi	1925	J. Cyreck, München
Bye-Lo-Baby	1922	Geo. Borgfeldt & Co., Berlin

C

Caho	1925	Canzler & Hofmann, Sonneberg
Cama	-	Armand Marseille, Sonneberg
Campbell Kids	1911	Josef Sükind, Hamburg
Campbell Kids	1911	Carl Harmus, Sonneberg
Campbell-Puppen	1926	Otto Sauerteig, Neustadt
Caprice	1922	Emil Bauersachs, Sonneberg
Carmencita	1912	Arthur Schoenau, Sonneberg
Carl	-	Kämmer & Reinhardt, Waltershausen
Casadora	1921	Huttinger & Buschor, Behringersdorf
Cebaso	1926	Carl Beck & Alfred Schulze, Ohrdruf
Cecille	-	Martin Eichhorn, Sonneberg
Cefer	1924	C.F. Reinhardt, Coburg
Celebrate	-	Georg Borgfeldt & Co., Berlin
Cellulit	1909	Kley & Hahn, Ohrdruf
Cellulobrin	1909	Franz Schmidt & Co., Georgenthal
Cellunova	1913	Kley & Hahn, Ohrdruf
Century Doll Co	-	J.D. Kestner jr., Waltershausen
Certa	1931	Adolf Wislizenus, Waltershausen
Chantecler Puppen	1911	Geo. Borgfeldt & Co., Berlin
Chantecler Puppen	1911	Henze & Steinhäuser, Gehren
Chantecler Puppen	1911	Leven & Sprenger, Sonneberg

Mark- or article	=	Applied or used by the firm
Chantecler Puppen	1911	Wilhelm Strunz, Nürnberg
Charakterpuppe	1909	Kämmer & Reinhardt, Waltershausen
Charlie Carrot	1928	Geo. Borgfeldt & Co., Berlin
Chondrogen	1912	Max Räder, Sonneberg
Chubby	-	Louis Wolf & Co., Berlin
Cinderella Baby	1897	C.M. Bergmann sen., Waltershausen
Cleo	1926	Bayerische Celluloidwarenfabrik, Nürnberg
Columbia	1912	Armand Marseille, Köppelsdorf
Columbia	1912	C.M. Bergmann, Sonneberg
Coumbia	1912	Carl Hartmann, Neustadt
Columbia	1912	Geo. Borgfeldt & Co., Berlin
Com-A-Long	1921	Geo. Borgfeldt & Co., Berlin
Coquette	1914	Gebr. Heubach, Lichte
Cornoulioud-Doll	1913	Max Handwerck, Waltershausen
Cupid	1908	M. Kohnstamm & Co., Fürth
Cupido	1913	Karl Standfuss, Deuben

D

DADA	-	Hermsdorfer Celluloidwarenfabrik
Daheim	1919	Carl Hartmann, Neustadt
Dainty May	1923	Demalcol, Catterfeld
Dainty Serien	-	Edmund Knoch, Mönchröden
Daisy	1903	Geo. Borgfeldt & Co., Berlin
Daisy	1903	Edmond Ulrich Steiner, Sonneberg
DALABA	1931	Arthur Schoenau, Sonneberg
Das deutsche Kind	1929	Käthe Kruse Werkstätten, Bad Kösen
Darling	-	Strobel & Wilken, Sonneberg
Das kriechende Baby	1911	Kley & Hahn, Ohrdruf
Das lachende Baby	1931	Arthur Schoenau, Sonneberg
Das lebende Baby	1912	Julius Henschel, Berlin
Das Neugeborene	1925	Gustav Schmey, Sonneberg
Das strampelnde Baby	1911	Kley & Hahn, Ohrdruf
Das süße Trudel-chen	1905	Johannes Kriege, Magdeburg
Das Riesenbaby	1912	Kley & Hahn, Ohrdruf
Das Träumerchen	1929	Käthe Kruse Werkstätten, Bad Kösen

Mark- or article	=	Applied or used by the firm
Daumenlutscher	-	Richard Scherzer, Sonneberg
Daumenlutscher	1929	Carl Heumann, Sonneberg
Daumenlutscher	1929	Huttinger & Buschor, Behringersdorf
DEKAWE	1924	Carl Herrmann, Potsdam
DEKAWE	1924	Deutsche Kolonial-Kapok-Werke AG., Berlin
Delly	-	Delly Puppenfabrik, Stuttgart
Der Bösewicht	1916	Koenig & Wernicke, Waltershausen
Der deutsche Michel	1925	Oscar Kirchner, Schalkau
Der heitere Fridolin	-	Fleischmann & Bloedel, Nürnberg
Der kleine Hansi	1925	Wagner & Zetsche, Ilmenau
Der kleine Spatz	1926	Bayerische Celluloidwarenfabrik, Nürnberg
Der kleine Mensch	-	Mittelland Gummiwerke, Hannover
Der rosige Liebling	-	Kämmer & Reinhardt, Waltershausen
Der Schelm	1908	Kämmer & Reinhardt, Waltershausen
Der Unart	1916	Kämmer & Reinhardt, Waltershausen
Dewey, Admiral	1897	Cuno & Otto Dressel, Sonneberg
Dewey Doll	1899	Gebr. Süßengut, Neustadt
Diana	1903	Alfred Heller, Meiningen
Didi	1923	Geo. Borgfeldt & Co., Berlin
Didi	1923	Alt, Beck & Gottschalck, Nauendorf
Die kleine Hansi	1925	Wagner & Zetsche, Ilmenau
Die kleine Range	1916	Koenig & Wernicke, Walterhausen
Die Kokette	1907	Kämmer & Reinhardt, Waltershausen
Die Potsdamer Soldaten	1915	Käthe Kruse Werkstätten, Bad Kösen
Dollarprinzessin	1927	Dr. Dora Petzold, Berlin
Dolly Dimple	1907	Hamburger & Co., Berlin
Dolly Dimple	1913	Butler Brothers, Sonneberg
Dolly Mine	1911	Gans & Seyfarth, Waltershausen
Dolly Pat Travels	1914	Richard Scherzer, Sonneberg
Dolly Varden	1895	Cuno & Otto Dressel, Sonneberg
Dolly Varden	-	Butler Brothers, Sonneberg
Dora	-	Porzellanfabrik Rauenstein
Dorothy	-	Butler Brothers, Sonneberg
Dotty	1913	Geo. Borgfeldt & Co., Berlin
Dreso-Puppe	1926	Fritz Dressel, Sonneberg

Mark- or article	=	Applied or used by the firm
Dry climate	1911	Geo. Borgfeldt & Co., Berlin
Duchess	-	Armand Marseille, Köppelsdorf
Duchess	-	Geo. Borgfeldt & Co., Berlin
Durabel	1909	Kley & Hahn, Ohrdruf

E

EBASO	1930	Emil Bauersachs, Sonneberg
ECCO	1926	Eckstein & Co., Sonneberg
Eclaireur	1914	Gutmann & Schiffnie, Nürnberg
Edelkind	1918	Hugo Wiegand, Waltershausen
Eden Bebe	1890	Fleischmann & Bloedel, Nürnberg
Edith	-	Butler Brothers, Sonneberg
Einco	-	Eisenmann & Co., Fürth
Eleonore	-	Simon & Halbig, Gräfenhain
Eleonore	-	C.M. Bergmann, Sonneberg
Elfe	1922	Gans & Seyfarth, Waltershausen
Elfenhaut	1925	Amberg & Hergershausen, Berlin
Elfen-Puppe	1924	Koenig & Wernicke, Waltershausen
Eli	-	Ernst Liebermann, Neustadt
Elie	1928	Karl Müller & Co., Effelder
Elite	1915	Max Handwerck, Waltershausen
ELLAR	1925	Armand Marseille, Köppelsdorf
Elsa	-	Unbekannt
Elsie	1898	Geo. Borgfeldt & Co., Berlin
EMASO	-	Ma.E. Maar, Mönchröden
Erfordia	1922	Otto Reipert, Erfurt
Erika	1922	Simon & Halbig, Gräfenhain
Erika	1922	Carl Hartmann, Neustadt
Esco	1922	Sommer & Co., Berlin
Escora	1926	Eduard Schmidt, Coburg
Esther	-	Butler Brothers, Sonneberg
Esy	1919	E. Suchetzsky, Berlin
Ethel	-	Butler Brothers, Sonneberg
Excelsior	-	Louis Wolf & Co., Sonneberg
Excelsior	-	Heinrich Schmuckler, Liegnitz
Excelsior	-	J.D.Kestner jr., Waltershausen

F

Mark- or article		Applied or used by the firm
Fahn	-	Reupke & Co., Sonneberg
Fahn	1920	F.A. Heubach Nachf., Sonneberg
Fancora-Wunder-baby	1927	Franz Angermüller, Coburg
Fany	1912	Armand Marseille, Köppelsdorf
Fanny	-	Armand Marseille, Köppelsdorf
Fat Baby	-	J.D. Kestner jr., Waltershausen
Favorite Saxonia	1910	Nöckler & Tittel, Schneeberg
Feldgrauen	1915	Käthe Kruse Werkstätten, Bad Kösen
Feldgrauen	1915	Kley & Hahn, Ohrdruf
Feldgrauen	1915	Margarete Steiff, Giengen
Fema	1922	Beck & Co., Waltershausen
Fifth Ave Doll	1903	Cuno & Otto Dressel, Sonneberg
Fingy-Legs-The-Tiny Tot	1912	Geo. Borgfeldt & Co., Berlin
Flags Of All Nations	1899	Cuno & Otto Dressel, Sonneberg
Flora	1924	Eisfelder Puppenfabrik, Eisfeld
Florence	-	Butler Brothers, Sonneberg
Floresta	1920	Scheyer & Co., Nürnberg
Florigotto	1921	Florig & Otto, Dresden
Florodora	1901	Armand Marseille, Köppelsdorf
Forodora	1901	Geo. Borgfeldt & Co., Berlin
Flossie Fischer`s Own Doll	1921	Geo. Borgfeldt & Co., Berlin
Fluffy Ruffles	1907	Max Schellhorn, Sonneberg
Friedel	-	E.W. Matthes, Berlin
Fridolin	-	Fleischmann & Bloedel, Nürnberg
Fritz	-	Emil Pfeiffer, Wien
Frivona	-	F. Voigt Nachf., Sonneberg
Frizzi	-	John Hess, Hamburg

G

Mark- or article		Applied or used by the firm
Gee Gee Dolly	1914	E.J. Horsman C., New York
Gehrenia	1921	Henze & Steinhäuser, Gehren
Geo	-	Gebr. Eckardt, Oberlind

Mark- or article	=	Applied or used by the firm
Georgi	1924	Eleonore Georgi, Koblenz
GESUE	-	Gebr. Süßenguth, Neustadt
GETE-Puppe	-	Gustav Thiele, Waltershausen
Gibson Girl	-	Margarete Steiff, Giengen
Gibson Girl	-	J.D. Kestner jr., Waltershausen
Gladdie	1929	Geo. Borgfeldt & Co., Berlin
Globe-Babies	1899	Carl Hartmann, Neustadt
Gloriosa	-	J.D. Kestner jr., Waltershausen
Goldherz	1908	Bruno Schmidt, Waltershausen
Goldstern	-	Adolf Hülß, Waltershausen
Granitol	1905	Carl Hoffmeister, Sonneberg
Graziella Puppen	1923	Max Sachs, Charlottenburg
Grecon-Puppe	1919	Grete Cohn, Berlin
Gretchen	1910	Adolf Wislizenus, Waltershausen
Gretchen	1909	Kämmer & Reinhardt, Waltershausen
Grete	1925	Porzellanfabrik Mengersgereuth
Gummoid	1901	Nöckler & Tittel, Schneeberg
Guschi	1922	Gutmann & Schiffnie, Sonneberg
Gymnastik Doll	1930	Albin Heß, Schalkau

H

Habeka	1930	Hermann von Berg, Köppelsdorf
Hafraco Puppe	1922	Schöffl & Co., Berlin
Hako	1925	Hachmeister & Co., Sonneberg
Haliso	-	Heinrich Liebermann, Sonneberg
Hanco	1921	Hahn & Co., Nürnberg
Handora	1922	Ohrdrufer Handelsgesellschaft
Hanka	1925	Gebr. Pfeiffer, Köppelsdorf
Hanna	1920	Arthur Schoenau, Sonneberg
Hannelore	-	Hermann Pensky, Coburg
Hans	1909	Kämmer & Reinhardt, Waltershausen
Hans	1925	Porzellanfabrik Mengersgereuth
Hansa	1902	Carl Hartmann, Neustadt
Hansa-Puppe	1925	W. Reinick, Hamburg
Hänsel & Gretel	1906	Moritz Pappe, Liegnitz
Hansi	1925	Wagner & Zetsche, Ilmenau
Happifat	1914	Geo. Borgfeldt & Co., Berlin
Happy Hooligan	1923	Geo. Borgfeldt & Co., Berlin

Mark- or article	=	Applied or used by the firm
Hapusa	1927	Hermann Hachmeister, Sonneberg
Harald	1915	Wagner & Zetsche, Ilmenau
Haralit	1916	Wagner & Zetsche, Ilmenau
Hawadit	1920	Hammer Munitionswerk, Wallendorf
Heinerle	-	Helene Haeusler, Sonneberg
Hedi	1924	S. Schwerin Nachf., Breslau
Heico	1925	M. Heider & Co., Nürnberg
Heio-Beio	1927	Richard Scherzer, Sonneberg
Heiterer Fridolin	1922	Fleischmann & Bloedel, Nürnberg
Helen	-	Unbekannt/Butler Brothers, Sonneberg
Helgünith	1925	Oskar Günthel, Gräfenroda
Henny	1922	Böhnke & Zimmermann, Königsberg
Henny Puppe	1923	Loetel & Co., Braunschweig
Henza	1927	Henze & Steinhäuser, Gehren
Herka	1914	Martha Köllner, Ilmenau
Hercules	1907	Josef Deuerlein, Nürnberg
Herz	1910	Bruno Schmidt, Waltershausen
Herzchen	1926	Albert Müller, Nossen
Herzi	-	Porzellanfabrik Mengersgereuth
Herzkäferchen	1926	Bauer & Richter, Stadtroda
Herzlieb	1914	Scherzer & Fischer, Sonneberg
Herzlieb	1913	Hugo Wiegand, Waltershausen
Herzpuppen	1923	Herzpuppen-Fabrik, Berlin
Hesli	1921	Heinrich Schmuckler, Liegnitz
Hewika	1925	Hertwig & Co., Katzhütte
Hexe	-	Unbekannt
Hilda	1914	J.D. Kestner jr., Waltershausen
Hi-Way Henry	1927	Geo. Borgfeldt & Co., Berlin
Hochtourist	1907	Mathilde Sehm, Guben
Holzmasse	1875	Cuno & Otto Dressel, Sonneberg
Holzmasse	1895	Julius Dorst, Sonneberg
Huberta	-	Emil Pfeiffer, Wien
Hubsy-Puppen	1926	Emil Pfeiffer, Wien
Huddi-Figuren	-	Bruno Schmidt, Waltershausen

I

IGES	1914	J.G. Escher & Sohn, Sonneberg
IGODI	1925	Kohl & Wengenroth, Offenbach

Mark- or article		= Applied or used by the firm
Illco	1927	Carl A. Illing & Co., Sonneberg
Imperial	1901	Hamburger & Co., Sonneberg
Instructible Heads	-	Cuno & Otto Dressel, Sonneberg
Inge	1916	Wagner & Zetsche, Ilmenau
Iris	1924	Iris Beaumont, Berlin
Irvington	1910	Geo. Borgfeldt & Co., Berlin
I-We-Em	1924	Ines Wetzel, Berlin

J

Jackie Coogan	1924	Harburger Gummiwaren-Fabrik
Jackie Coogan	1924	Fleischmann & Bloedel, Nürnberg
Jackie Coogan	1925	Gustav Förster, Neustadt
Japanese Baby	-	M. Kohnstamm & Co., Fürth
JDEN	1913	Josef Deuerlein Nachf., Nürnberg
Jing-Go-Ring-Doll	1913	Fritz Lutz, Sonneberg
Jointed Doll	-	Gans & Seyfarth, Waltershausen
Jointed Doll	1916	C.M. Bergmann, Waltershausen
Jointed Doll	-	Adolf Wislizenus, Waltershausen
Jose	-	Johannes Sauerteig, Sonneberg
Jubilee Doll	-	Strobel & Wilken, Sonneberg
Juno	1903	Karl Standfuss, Deuben
Just me	1924	Armand Marseille, Köppelsdorf
Just me	1924	Geo. Borgfeldt & Co., Berlin
Jutta	1907	Cuno & Otto Dressel, Sonneberg

K

KALUTU	-	Carl Kalbitz, Sonneberg
Keep Smiling	1925	Elise Israel, Zittau
Kewpie	-	Hermann Voigt, Schaala
Kewpie	-	Carl Völker, Sonneberg
Kewpie	-	Karl Standfuss, Deuben
Kewpie	1913	Geo. Borgfeldt & Co., Berlin
Kewpie	1913	J.D. Kestner jr., Waltershausen
Kewpie	1913	Margarete Steiff, Giengen
Kid Doll	-	Carl Hoffmeister, Sonneberg
Kiddiejoy	1925	Armand Marseille, Köppelsdorf
Kidolin	-	Carl Hoffmeister, Sonneberg

Mark- or article	=	Applied or used by the firm
Kidlyne Doll	-	Carl Hoffmeister, Sonneberg
Kidette Doll	-	Carl Hoffmeister, Sonneberg
Kindertraum	1930	Otto Gans, Waltershausen
Kissie	-	Cuno & Otto Dressel, Sonneberg
Kleeblatt	-	Moritz Pappe, Liegnitz
Klein Mammy	1925	Kämmer & Reinhardt, Waltershausen
Kleiner Sonnen-chein	1922	Catterfelder Puppenfabrik
Kleiner Spatz	1926	Bayerische Celluloidwarenfabrik, Nürnberg
Knopf im Ohr	1905	Margarete Steiff, Giengen
Königskinder	1912	Koenig & Wernicke, Waltershausen
KO-KO	1925	Geo. Borgfeldt & Co., Berlin
Kolundro	1913	Martin Winterbauer, Nürnberg
Kolundro	1925	Josef Deuerlein Nachf., Nürnberg
Kolundro	1913	Kohler & Rosenwald, Nürnberg
Kowenko	1925	Kohl & Wengenroth, Offenbach
Kronen Puppe	1915	J.D. Kestner jr., Waltershausen
Künstlerkopf	-	Schoenau & Hoffmeister, Burggrub

L

La Belle	1914	Heinrich Handwerck, Waltershausen
La Bonita	1914	Heinrich Handwerck, Waltershausen
La Superba	1906	Max Oscar Arnold, Neustadt
Lehowa	1922	Lehowa, Sonneberg
Lieb Edelkind	-	Hugo Wiegand, Waltershausen
Liebling lernt laufen	1927	Kämmer & Reinhardt, Waltershausen
Liliput	1902	Carl Geyer, Sonneberg
Lilly	-	Armand Marseille, Köppelsdorf
Linon	1895	Isidor Eisenstaedt & Co., Waltershausen
Linon	1895	Hermann Landshut & Co., Waltershausen
Lisa	1926	Elise Israel, Zittau
Lithoid	1901	Nöckler & Tittel, Schneeberg
Little Annie Rooney	1926	Geo. Borgfeldt & Co., Berlin
Little Bright Eyes	1912	Geo. Borgfeldt & Co., Berlin
Little sister	1914	Geo. Borgfeldt & Co., Berlin

Mark- or article	=	Applied or used by the firm
Little Snookums, the newlywed`s Baby	1910	Max Fr. Schellhorn, Sonneberg
Little Sunshine	1923	Catterfelder Puppenfabrik
Little Sunshine	1926	Demalcol GmbH., Catterfeld
Little Sweetheart	1902	Max Illfelder, Fürth
Lona-Künstler-puppe	-	A. Schmidt, Dresden
Lopto	1924	Thüringer Puppen- und Spielwaren-Export, Berlin
Lori	1910	Swaine & Co., Hüttensteinach
Lotte	-	Victor Steiner, Sonneberg
Lotte	-	Cuno & Otto Dressel, Sonneberg
Lotti	-	Heinrich Handwerck, Waltershausen
Lucille	-	Martin Eichhorn, Sonneberg
Lullabye Baby	-	Martin Eichhorn, Sonneberg
Luta	1930	Eg.M. Luthardt, Steinach
Lyro	1923	Rolfes & Co., Berlin
Lyro	1925	Franz Volpert, Charlottenburg

M

Maba Künstler-puppe	1927	Max A. Barnikol, Sonneberg
Mabel	-	Armand Marseille, Köppelsdorf
Mabel	-	Butler Brothers, Sonneberg
Madame Butterfly	1913	Max Handwerck, Waltershausen
Mafuka	1925	Otto Scheyer & Co., Nürnberg
Majestic	1902	Ernst Ulrich Steiner, Sonneberg
Majestic	1907	Kley & Hahn, Ohrdruf
Majestic	1902	Kämmer & Reinhardt, Waltershausen
Mamas Herzensschatz	1927	Friedrichsrodaer Puppenfabrik
Mammy	1925	Kämmer & Reinhardt, Waltershausen
Maquette	1903	Pulvermacher & Westram, Sonneberg
Maquette	1880	Wilhelm Simon, Hildburghausen
Maria	1925	Strasserpuppen-Werkstätten, Berlin
Marie	1909	Kämmer & Reinhardt, Waltershausen
Margret	-	Armand Marseille, Köppelsdorf

Mark- or article	=	Applied or used by the firm
Margret	-	Cuno & Otto Dressel, Sonneberg
Marion	-	Butler Brothers, Sonneberg
Marta	1908	Carl Hartmann, Neustadt
Marvel	1899	J.D. Kestner jr., Waltershausen
Marvel	1899	Butler Brothers, Sonneberg
Mausi	1908	Robert Carl, Köppelsdorf
Maya	1926	Geschw. Heinrich, Nürnberg
Max und Moritz	1910	Kilian Cramer, Grobreitenbach
Max und Moritz	1912	Theodor Recknagel, Alexandrinenthal
Max und Moritz	1911	Margarete Steiff, Giengen
Max und Moritz	1907	Mathilde Sehm, Guben
Max und Moritz	1913	Kämmer & Reinhardt, Waltershausen
Max und Moritz	1913	Kley & Hahn, Ohrdruf
Max und Moritz	1913	J.D. Kestner jr., Waltershausen
Maxi	-	Max Beuster, Kiel
May Blossom	1923	Demalcol, Catterfeld
May Blossom	-	Alfred Lange, Friedrichsroda
McKinley	1897	Cuno & Otto Dressel, Sonneberg
Mein Augenstern	1914	Paul Zierow, Berlin
Mein Einziger	-	Kley & Hahn, Ohrdruf
Mein Glückskind	1919	Adolf Wislizenus, Waltershausen
Mein Goldherz	1910	Bruno Schmidt, Waltershausen
Mein Goldstern	1926	C.M. Bergmann, Waltershausen
Mein Goldstern	-	Adolf Hülß, Waltershausen
Mein Herz`l	1910	Catterfelder Puppenfabrik
Mein Herzenskind	1929	Wilhelm Buschow, Dresden
Mein kleiner Liebling	1927	Kämmer & Reinhardt, Walterhausen
Mein kleiner Schlingel	1926	Bauer & Richter, Stadtroda
Mein Kleines	1911	Kämmer & Reinhardt, Waltershausen
Mein liebes Kind	1925	Alfred Heller, Waltershausen
Mein Liebling	1902	Kämmer & Reinhardt, Waltershausen
Mein Lieblingsbaby	1914	Kämmer & Reinhardt, Waltershausen
Mein Nesthäckchen	-	Adolf Hülß, Waltershausen
Mein neuer Liebling	1916	Kämmer & Reinhardt, Waltershausen

Mark- or article	=	Applied or used by the firm
Mein rosiger Liebling	1931	Kämmer & Reinhardt, Waltershausen
Mein Sonnenschein	1910	Catterfelder Puppenfabrik
Mein Stern	1925	Henriette Dunker, Hamburg
Mein Stolz	1914	Koenig & Wernicke, Waltershausen
Mein süßer Liebling	1912	Kämmer & Reinhardt, Waltershausen
Mein süßer Schlingel	1926	Rodaer Puppenfabrik Bauer & Richter
Mein Wunschkind	1934	Arthur Schoenau, Sonneberg
Mein Ziergold	-	Elisabeth Schwarz, Gotha
Meine Einzige	1910	Kley & Hahn, Ohrdruf
Meine Goldperle	1925	Alfred Heller, Waltershausen
Meine Goldsternchen	-	Bruno Schmidt, Waltershausen
Melitta	1922	Edmund Edelmann, Sonneberg
Merry Widow	1909	Max Illfelder, Fürth
Mew Puss	1925	Johann Heinrich Kletzin & Co., Coburg
Mi Encanto	1930	Seligmann & Mayer, Sonneberg
Mia	1925	M. Hecht, Nietleben
Miblu	1925	Kämmer & Reinhardt, Waltershausen
Miblu	1925	Rheinische Gummi- und Celluloidfabrik, Mannheim
Miblu	1925	Koenig & Wernicke, Waltershausen
Michel	1911	A. Michaelis, Rauenstein
Michu	1914	Fleischmann & Blodel, Nürnberg
Miles	1897	Cuno & Otto Dressel, Sonneberg
Mimi	1922	Geo. Borgfeldt & Co., Berlin
Mimi	1922	Alt, Beck & Gottschalck, Nauendorf
Mimosa	1924	Mimosa, Ochenbruck bei Nürnberg
Mine	1922	Edmund Edelmann, Sonneberg
Minverva	1900	Buschow & Beck, Nossen
Minnie Spinach	1928	Geo. Borgfeldt & Co., Berlin
Miss Elisabeth	1924	Zum Puppenheim, Sonneberg
Miss Millionaire	1913	Butler Brothers, Sonneberg
Miss Royal	1924	Zum Puppenheim, Sonneberg
Mit dem Goldreif	1923	Ilse Müller, Berlin
MOA	-	Max Oscar Arnold, Neustadt

Mark- or article		= Applied or used by the firm
Mobi	1921	Hermann Schiemer, Nürnberg
Moko	-	M. Kohnstamm & Co., Fürth
Mona	1922	Edmund Edelmann, Sonneberg
Mona Lisa	1914	Gutmann & Schiffnie, Sonneberg
Mon Petit Coeur	-	Bruno Schmidt, Waltershausen
Monte-Carlo-Genre	1910	Galluba & Hofmann, Ilmenau
Monty	1929	Jos. Süsskind, Hamburg
Mosca	1923	Max Mocsardini & Co., Berlin
Mothers Darling	1910	M. Kohnstamm & Co., Fürth
MÜKA	-	Müller & Kaltwasser, Rauenstein
Muing	1928	W. Goebel, Sonneberg
Muk	1926	Elise Israel, Zittau
Muschi	1928	Martha Lehmann, Dresden
Mutzipuppe	1925	Ch. Kirchoff, Berlin
My Annemarie	1923	Wilhelm Follender, Düsseldorf
My Cherub	1924	Arthur Schoenau, Sonneberg
My Companion	-	Armand Marseille, Köppelsdorf
My Companion	-	Louis Wolf & Co., Sonneberg
My Darling	1906	Kämmer & Reinhardt, Waltershausen
My Dearie	1922	Otto Gans, Waltershausen/ Wiesenthal,
My Dearie	1922	Schindel & Kallenberg, Waltershausen
My Dream Baby	1925	Armand Marseille, Köppelsdorf
My Dream Baby	1925	Arranbee Doll & Co., New York
My Darling	-	Kämmer & Reinhardt, Waltershausen
My Fairy	1922	Seyfarth & Reinhardt, Waltershausen
My Girlie	1912	Geo. Borgfeldt & Co., Berlin
My Honey	1922	Eduard Römhild, Sonneberg
My Honey-Dolls	1922	Nordicus Colonda Werke, Sonneberg
My little Darling	1910	Hermann Kröning, Gotha
My Pearl	1921	Hermann Steiner, Sonneberg
My Pet	1905	Buschow & Beck, Nossen
My Playmate	-	Armand Marseille, Köppelsdorf
My Playmate	1903	Geo. Borgfeldt & Co., Berlin
My Playmate	-	Koenig & Wernicke, Waltershausen
My Playmate	-	Kämmer & Reinhardt, Waltershausen
My Sweetheart	1902	B. Illfelder & Co., Fürth
My Sweetheart	-	Adolf Wislizenus, Waltershausen
My Queen Doll	1921	Gebr. Ohlhaver, Sonneberg

Mark- or article	=	Applied or used by the firm
N		
Nanette	1926	M. Kohnstamm & Co., Fürth
Natura	1927	P. Hunaeus, Hannover
Naughty	1920	Kämmer & Reinhardt, Waltershausen
Nesthäkchen	1927	Adolf Hülß, Waltershausen
New Born Babe	1926	Louis Amberg & Son, Sonneberg
Niddy Impekoven	1919	Selma von Hasberg, Frankfurt
Nobbikid	-	Armand Marseille, Köppelsdorf
Nobbikid	1915	Geo. Borgfeldt & Co., Berlin
Nobrake	1909	Vereinigte Spielwarenfabriken, Waltershausen
Nobrake	1909	Schmidt & Goerke, Waltershausen
Nollipolli	1930	Kämmer & Reinhardt, Waltershausen
Nora	1922	Nora Puppenfabrik, Sonneberg
Noris	1905	Carl Debes & Sohn, Hof
Noris	-	Bayerische Celluloidwarenfabrik, Nürnberg
Norma	-	Porzellanfabrik Limbach
O		
Oco	1925	Offenbach & Co., Nürnberg
Oga	1925	Otto Gans, Waltershausen
Old Glory	1902	Adolf Wislizenus, Waltershaus
Old Rip	-	Unbekannt
Olympia	-	Unbekannt
Ormond	1923	D.H. Wagner & Sohn, Grünhainichen
Our Baby	1916	Louis Wolf & Co., Sonneberg
Our Fairy	-	Louis Wolf & Co., Sonneberg
Our Pet	1930	Gebr. Eckardt, Oberlind
Our Pet	-	Armand Marseille, Köppelsdorf
P		
Paddy Potato	1927	Geo. Borgfeldt & Co., Berlin
Paladin Babies	1903	Carl Hartmann, Neustadt
Paladin Babies	1903	Kämmer & Reinhardt, Waltershausen
Pansy	1921	Geo. Borgfeldt & Co., Berlin
PAMA-Stimmen	-	G. Herold, Neustadt
Panta	1929	Kämmer & Reinhardt, Waltershausen
Patent-Head	1879	Fritz Vogel, Sonneberg

Mark- or article		= Applied or used by the firm
Patent-Lederbebe	-	vermutlich Wagner & Zetsche, Ilmenau
Patentmasse	1888	L.R. Hörchner & Co., Friedrichsrode
Patentmasse	1890	Kämmer & Reinhardt, Waltershausen
Papp-Head	1908	Simon Junghans, Rittersgrün
Pat-a-cake	1912	A. Luge & Co., Sonneberg
Peha	1928	P. Hunaeus, Hannover
Pehaco	-	Hermann Pensky, Coburg
Perfectolid	1934	Arthur Schoenau, Sonneberg
Perlico-Perlaco	1910	Fleischmann & Bloedel, Nürnberg
PESO	1922	Paul Schmidt, Sonneberg
Pet Names	-	Butler Brothers, Sonneberg
Peter	1909	Kämmer & Reinhardt, Waltershausen
Peter Pan Playtoys	1907	M.Fr. Schellhorn, Sonneberg
Phyllis Doll	1923	Schmidt & Nüchter, Gröfenroda
Phoenix	1924	Harburger Gummiwaren-Fabrik
PIGO	1924	Puppenindustrie Gotha
Pioneer	1910	Carl Hartmann, Neustadt
Pipa	1925	D.H. Wagner & Sohn, Grünhainichen
Pirola	1925	D.H. Wagner & Sohn, Grünhainichen
Pirouette	1925	D.H. Wagner & Sohn, Grünhainichen
Pfiffikus	1912	Koenig & Wernicke, Waltershausen
Pfiffikus	1913	Franz Kiesewetter, Neustadt
Playmate	1920	Emil Bauersachs, Sonneberg
Plombe in der Hand	-	Rudolf Säuberlich, Berlin
Pola Puppen	1923	Thüringer Puppenindustrie, Gotha
Polait	1902	M. Polack, Waltershausen
Poppy Dolls	1912	Cuno & Otto Dressel, Sonneberg
Porzellanit	1929	Kämmer & Reinhardt, Waltershausen
Potsdamer Soldaten	1915	Käthe Kruse Werkstätten, Bad Kösen
Pauline	-	Butler Brothers, Sonneberg
Powerful Katrinka	1923	Geo. Borgfeldt & Co., Berlin
Primrose	1922	Waltershäuser Puppenfabrik
Primula	1923	Thüringer Puppen- und Spielwaren-Export, Berlin
Princess	-	Armand Marseille, Köppelsdorf
Princess	-	Kley & Hahn, Ohrdruf
Princess	1909	Geo. Borgfeldt & Co., Berlin

Mark- or article	=	Applied or used by the firm
Princess Elizabeth	1932	Arthur Schoenau, Sonneberg
Princess Elizabeth	1930	Christian Hopf, Neustadt
Prinzess Bett	-	M. Kohnstamm & Co., Fürth
Prinzess Sibylla	1932	Hermann Eckstein, Neustadt
Prinzessin Wunderhold	1912	Arthur Schoenau, Sonneberg
Prize Baby	1914	Geo. Borgfeldt & Co., Berlin
Puck	1923	Florig & Otto, Dresden
Puppe der Zukunft	1904	Gebr. Süssenguth, Neustadt
Puspi	1925	H. Wordtmann, Hamburg

Q

Queen Louise	1910	Armand Marseille, Köppelsdorf
Queen Quality	1910	Adolf Wislizenus, Waltershausen

R

Racker	1919	Gans & Seyfarth, Waltershausen
rar/use	-	Adolf Wislizenus, Waltershausen
Reformpuppe	1904	Georg Becker, Hagen
Reg`lar Fellars	1923	Geo. Borgfeldt & Co., Berlin
Reso	1930	Schilling & Zitzmann, Sonneberg
Revalo	1919	Carl Harmus jr., Sonneberg
Revalo	1919	Gebr. Ohlhaver, Sonneberg
Revalo	1919	Ernst Heubach, Köppelsdorf
Rinaldo	1927	Berthold Helk, Neustadt
Rita	-	Porzellanfabrik Limbach
Rock-A-Bye-Baby	1925	Cuno & Otto Dressel, Sonneberg
Roli Cellowachs	1929	Kämmer & Reinhardt, Waltershausen
Rollschuhläufer	1911	Bernhnard Zehner, Schalkau
Roma	1913	Plass & Roessner, Böhmen
Roscamp-Puppen-Fantasien	1926	Katarina Roscamp, Berlin
Roschco	1925	Robert Schneider, Coburg
Rosebud	-	Armand Marseille, Köppelsdorf
Rosebud	-	M. Illfelder & Co., Fürth
Rose-Puppe	1925	F. Welsch, Berlin
Rosi	1929	Kämmer & Reinhardt, Waltershausen

Rotkäppchen	1925	Rotkäppchen GmbH., Berlin
Rotkäppchen	1894	O. Ludwig, Gehren
Royal	-	J.D. Kestner jr, Waltershausen
Ruth	1922	Butler Brothers, Sonneberg
Ruthea-Puppen	-	Grete Ruhl, Leipzig

S

Sag' Schnucki zu mir	-	Wally Fischel, Berlin
Sam Boy	-	M. Kohnstamm & Co., Fürth
Sampson	1897	Cuno & Otto Dressel, Sonneberg
Santa	-	Simon & Halbig, Gräfenhain
Santa	1901	Hamburger & Co., Berlin
Schalk	1919	Gans & Seyfarth, Waltershausen
Schelmaugen	1927	Kämmer & Reinhardt, Waltershausen
Schieler	1921	August Friedrich Carl, Sonneberg
Schlenkerchen	1922	Käthe Kruse Werkstätten, Bad Kösen
Schneeflöckchen	-	Nöckler & Tittel, Schneeberg
Schneeglöckchen	-	Nöckler & Tittel, Schneeberg
Schneewittchen	1905	Kley & Hahn, Ohrdruf
Schwesterchen	-	Friedrichsrodaer Puppenfabrik
Seco	-	Strauss-Eckardt C., Inc. New York
Seco	-	Gebr. Eckardt, Oberlind
Shirley Temple	-	Armand Marseille, Köppelsdorf
Sico	1926	Eduard Schmidt, Coburg
Sicora	-	Löffler & Dill, Sonneberg
Sicora	1925	Eduard Schmidt, Coburg
Siegfried	-	J.D. Kestner jr., Waltershausen
Siha	1923	Simon Hahn, Zirndorf
Snookums	1910	Max Friedrich Schellhorn, Sonneberg
Sonnenpuppe	-	Welsch & Co., Sonneberg
Sonny Boy	1930	Hugo Wiegand, Waltershausen
South Sea Baby	-	A. Luge & Co., Sonneberg
Special	-	Adolf Wislizenus, Waltershausen
Special	-	Kley & Hahn, Ohrdruf
Spezial	-	C.M. Bergmann, Waltershausen
Spezial	-	F. Kuhles, Catterfeld
Stabil	1923	Robert Richter, Waltershausen

Mark- or article	=	Applied or used by the firm
Stabil	-	Emil Heyer & Co., Gräfenroda
Star	-	H. Eckstein, Neustadt
Stella	1920	J. Stellmacher, Steinheid
Storch	-	Schwäbische Celluloidwarenfabrik, Mengen
Strampelchen	1925	Edith Maus, Braunschweig
Strandfee	1923	'O. Eberwein & Co., Hamburg
Südsee-Baby	1928	A. Luge & Co., Sonneberg
Suck Thumb Baby	1929	Carl Heumann, Sonneberg
Sugar Plum	1925	Geo. Borgfeldt, & Co., Berlin
SUN	1922	Sigmund Ullmann, Nürnberg
Superba	-	Unbekannt
Superior	-	Georg Lutz, Sonneberg/Cuno & Otto
Superior	-	Dressel, Sonneberg/Müller & Strasburger, Sonneberg
Superior	-	Fleischmann & Co., Sonneberg
Superior	-	Heinrich Handwerck, Waltershausen
SUR	1923	Seyfarth & Reinhardt, Waltershausen
Susie	1924	Cuno & Otto Dressel, Sonneberg
Susi-Künstler-puppen	1923	Susi Künstlerpuppen, Stuttgart
Sweet Nell	1925	Hugo Wiegand, Waltershausen
Syco	-	Sieder & Co., Plauen

T

Taft	-	Unbekannt
Tago	1925	P. Bühl & Tannewitz, Gotha
Tausendschönchen	1910	Franz Schmidt & Co., Georgenthal
Tebu	-	Theodor Buschbaum, Wallendorf
Teenie Weenie	1922	Geo. Borgfeldt & Co., Berlin
Tessie	1925	M. Kohnstamm & Co., Fürth
The Base Ball Fan	1914	Max Friedrich Schellhorn, Sonneberg
The Dollar Princess	1909	Kley & Hahn, Ohrdruf
The Duchess Dressed Doll	1915	M. Kohnstamm & Co., Fürth
The Fairy Kid	1916	Peter Scherf, Sonneberg
The favorite Doll	-	Kämmer & Reinhardt, Waltershausen
The Flirt	1909	Kämmer & Reinhardt, Waltershausen

Mark- or article	=	Applied or used by the firm
The Handwercks Celebrated Doll	1922	Max Handwerck, Waltershausen
The International Doll	1898	Geo. Borgfeldt & Co., Berlin
The Jolly Jester	1927	Geo. Borgfeldt & Co., Berlin
The Skipper	1923	Geo. Borgfeldt & Co., Berlin
The Sonny Boy	-	M. Kohnstamm & Co., Fürth
Thuringia	1902	Carl Hartmann, Neustadt
Thuringia	-	Porzellanfabrik Thuringia
Thuringia	-	A. Luge & Co., Sonneberg
Thuringia	-	Thuringia AG., Hamburg
Thürpuin	1919	Thüringer Puppen Industrie, Waltershausen
Tiny Tots	1912	Geo. Borgfeldt & Co., Berlin
Tipple Topple	1916	Emil Pfeiffer, Wien
Tommy Turnip	1928	Geo. Borgfeldt & Co., Berlin
Tootsie	1906	Geo. Borgfeldt & Co., Berlin
Torino	1927	Berthold Helk, Neustadt
Tout Bois-All Wood	-	F.M. Schilling, Sonneberg
Trebor	-	Porzellanfabrik Mengersgereuth
Triumph Bebe	1902	Max Handwerck, Waltershausen
Trutzi	1922	Johannes Rejall, Dresden

U

Ulla Puppe	1922	Arthur Gotthelf, Remscheid
Ulla Puppe	1925	Schindhelm & Knauer, Sonneberg
Unbreakable	1876	Lambert & Samhammer, Sonneberg
Undine	-	> Mechanische Puppen
Unerreicht	1911	Adolph Harras Nachf., Grobreitenbach
Universal-Puppe	1890	Carl Bergner, Sonneberg
Uncle Sam	-	Cuno & Otto Dressel, Sonneberg
Unsere goldigen Drei	1913	Gebr. Heubach, Lichte
Unsere kleine Mammy	1925	Kämmer & Reinhardt, Waltershausen
Unsere süßen Mädel	1913	Gebr. Heubach, Lichte
Ursula	1913	E.W. Matthes, Berlin

Mark- or article	=	Applied or used by the firm
Uwanta	1899	Geo. Borgfeldt & Co., Berlin

V

Vanta Baby	-	ouis Amberg & Son, Sonneberg
Victoria Gelenk-puppe	1891	W.Fr. Schönhut, Hermannstadt
Viktoria	-	Julius Hering, Köppelsdorf
Viktoria	-	Cuno & Otto Dressel, Sonneberg
Viktoria	-	Heinrich Schmuckler, Liegnitz
Viktoriababies	-	G. Gebert, Berlin
Viktoria Luise	-	Carl Hartmann, Neustadt
Viola	1903	Hamburger & Co., Berlin
Viola	-	Schoenau & Hoffmeister, Burggrub
Violet	1927	Ernst Liebermann, Neustadt
Virginia Ginny for short	1927	Geo. Borgfeldt & Co., Berlin
Vivi	-	A. Gorrigenes & Co., Berlin
Vivi	-	Geo. Borgfeldt & Co., Berlin
Vöglein	1923	Emma Vogel, Berlin

W

Waldkind	1923	Vereinigung Finsterberger Puppenmacher
Walküre	1903	Kley & Hahn, Ohrdruf
Wally	-	Porzellanfabrik Limbach
Walpu	1925	Waltershäuser Puppenfabrik, Waltershausen
Walter	-	Kämmer & Reinhardt, Waltershausen
Waschecht	-	Cuno & Otto Dressel, Sonneberg
Waschecht	-	Kämmer & Reinhardt, Waltershausen
Waschecht	-	F.M. Schilling, Sonneberg
Washable Doll	-	Cuno & Otto Dressel, Sonneberg
Washable Doll	-	Kämmer & Reinhardt, Waltershausen
Washable Doll	-	Gebr. Haag, Sonneberg
Washable Doll	-	F.M. Schilling, Sonneberg
WEEGEM	-	W.G. Müller, Sonneberg
Weimarpüppchen	1923	Thüringer Stoffpuppen-Fabrik, Bad Berka
Weinende	-	Albert Schachne, Nürnberg
Weinende	-	Hertel, Schwab & Co., Stutzhausen

Whistling Jim	-	Gebr. Heubach, Lichte
Wide Awake	1914	Butler Brothers, Sonneberg
Wildfang	1929	Wagner & Zetsche, Ilmenau
Wimpern ges.gesch.	-	Simon & Halbig, Gräfenhain
Wimpern ges.gesch.	-	Heinrich Handwerck, Waltershausen
Wunderkind	1909	J.D. Kestner jr., Waltershausen

X

xtra	1902	Geo. Borgfeldt & Co., Berlin

DRP and DRGM Numbers of Trademarks or Stamps that can be found on bodies

Registration No.	DRP or DRGM	Year	Firm
5 332	DRGM	1892	Johannes Franz, Sonneberg
16 647	DRGM	1893	Hermann Wegner, Sonneberg
19 555	DRGM	1893	Franz Schmidt, Georgenthal
43 594	DRGM	1895	Richard Fröber, Hüttensteinach
46 547	DRP	1888	Josef Bergmann, Sonneberg
56 562	DRP	1890	Simon & Halbig, Gräfenhain
56 996	DRP	1890	Gottlieb Zinner, Schalkau
66 543	DRP	1892	Hermann Landshut & Co., Waltershausen
70 685	DRP	1893	J.D. Kestner jr., Waltershausen
78 281	DRP	1894	Reinhold Weingart jr. → Alt, Beck & Gottschalck and Franz Schmidt
100 279	DRP	1897	Heinrich Handwerck, Waltershausen
105 579	WZ	1908	Adolf Landsberger, Magdeburg
119 857	DRP	1900	Ferdinand Imhoff, Berlin
123 847	DRP	1901	Bernhard Heublein, Malmerz
132 410	DRGM	1900	Robert Carl, Köppelsdorf
EP 134 769	GM	1913	Armand Marseille, Köppelsdorf
160 638	DRGM	1901	Alfred Heller, Meiningen
193 440	DRGM	1903	Louis Stammberger, Schalkau
201 013	DRGM	1903	Louis Liebermann, Sonneberg
357 529	DRGM	1908	Hermann Wegner, Sonneberg
374 830	DRGM	1909	Armand Marseille, Köppelsdorf
374 831	DRGM	1909	Armand Marseille, Köppelsdorf
377 439	DRGM	1909	Armand Marseille, Köppelsdorf
421 481	DRGM	1911	Adolf Wislizenus, Waltershausen
441 857	DRGM	1910	F.M. Schilling, Sonneberg
442 910	DRGM	1910	Rudolf Walch, Unterweid
447 828	DRGM	1910	Rheinische Gummi- and Celluloid Fabrik, Mannheim-Neckarau
448 506	DRGM	1910	F.M. Schilling, Sonneberg
452 711	DRGM	1911	Wiesenthal, Schindel & Kallenberg, Waltershausen
459 754	DRP	1927	Hermann Steiner, Neustadt
486 986	DRGM	1911	Franz Belouscheck for Gebr. Heubach, Lichte
520 942	DRGM	1912	Alt, Beck & Gottschalck, Nauendorf
592 448	DRGM	1914	Karl Malter, Georgenthal
657 708	DRGM	1916	Wagner & Zetsche, Ilmenau
856 346	DRGM	1923	Johann Müller, Nürnberg
897 388	DRGM	1924	Louis Reber, Sonneberg
945 354	DRGM	1925	Priska Sander, Neustadt/Orla
954 642	DRGM	1926	Hermann Steiner, Neustadt/Coburg
1 125 389	DRGM	1930	Gebr. Süßenguth, Neustadt

1 Bayer. Celluloidwarenfabrik formerly Albert Wacker. **2** Iris Beaumont 1922. **3** Carl Bergner. **4** Rolf Berlich 1923. **5** Bing Künstlerpuppen 1925. **6** Geo. Borgfeldt & Co 1903. **7** Wilhelm Buschow 1929. **8** Robert Carl. **9** Catterfelder Puppenfabrik. **10** E. Dehler. **11** Theodor Degenring. **12** Creidlitz AG. **13** Josef Deuerlein 1907. **14+15** Julius Dorst. **16+17** Cuno & Otto Dressel. **18** Gebr. Eckardt after 1930. **19** Gebr. Eckardt for „SECO“ Strauss-Eckardt Co. NY. **20** Eisenmann & Co. 1895. **21** J. G. Escher & Sohn 1921. **22** Carl Feiler & Co. 1903. **23+24** Fischer, Naumann & Co. **25** Fleischmann & Craemer. **26** Florig & Otto 1920. **27** Gustav Förster. **28+29** Friedrichsrodaer Puppenfabrik. **30** Otto Gans 1930. **31** Carl Geyer & Co. 1895. **32** Georg Gebert. **33** Walter Goebel 1928. **34** Arthur Gotthelf 1922. **35+36** Ernst Großmann.

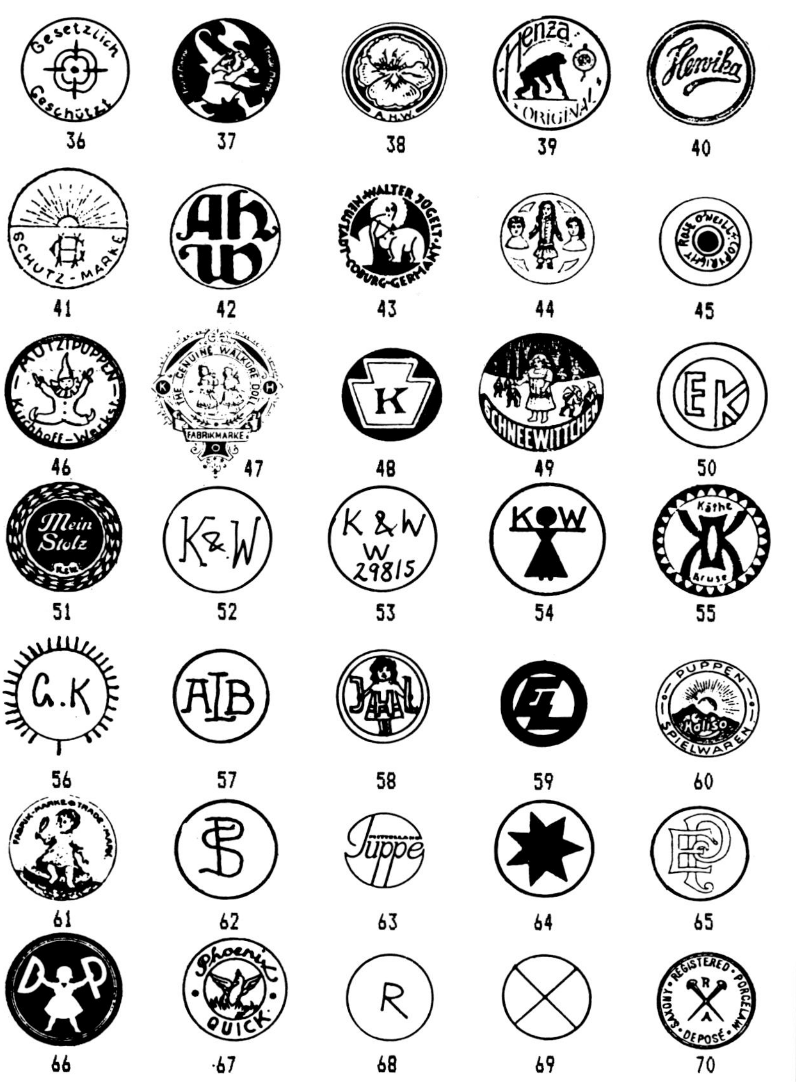

37 Erich Hachmeister 1908. **38** Adolf Heller 1925. **39** Henze & Steinhäuser 1925. **40** Hertwig & Co. 1925. **41** Gebr. Heubach. **42** Adolf Hülß 1925. **43** Walter Jügelt 1923. **44** J. D. Kestner jr. 1888. **45** Rose O'Neill. **46** Charlotte M. Kirchhoff 1925. **47** Kley & Hahn 1903. **48** Kley & Hahn 1904. **49** Kley & Hahn 1916. **50** Erich Kloetzer. **51** Koenig & Wernicke 1914. **52+53** Koenig & Wernicke. **54** Kohl & Wengenroth. **55** Käthe Kruse 1912. **56** Gebr. Kühnlenz AG. **57** Adolf Landsberger 1908. **58** H. J. Leven. **59** Ernst Liebermann. **60** Heinrich Liebermann 1927. **61** Loeffler & Dill. **62** Sonneberger Porzellanfabrik at the end 1940'. **63** Mittelland-Gummiwerke 1927. **64** Moritz Pappe 1907. **65** Emil Pfeiffer. **66** Dora Petzold 1920. **67** Phoenix Gummipuppen. **68+69** Porzellanfabrik Mengersgereuth. **70** Theodor Recknagel.

71 Curt F. Reinhardt, 1921. **72** Julius Rempel. **73** Scheyer & Co. 1920. **74** Franz Schmidt & Co. 1893. **75** Franz Schmidt & Co. ca. 1900. **76** Franz Schmidt & Co. 1907. **77** Paul Schmidt 1923. **78** Robert Schneider Coburg 1924. **79+80** Arthur Schoenau. **81** Emil Schwenk. **82** Sigismund Schwerin Nachf. 1923. **83** Seyfarth & Reinhardt 1923. **84** Margarete Steiff ca. 1898. **85** Margarete Steiff 1905. **86+87** Swaine & Co. **88** Thüringer Puppen- and Spielwaren-Export GmbH. 1923. **89** Gustav Thiele. **90** Friedr. Edmund Winkler 1899. **91** Adolf Wislizenus 1902. **92** Emil Wittzack. **93** A. C. Anger, Böhmen. **94** unknown. **95** Schmidt & Nüchter 1923. **96** Adolf Wislizenus. **97** von Hantelmann & Co., 1928. **98** Kloster Veilsdorf 1928. **99** Guido Knauth ca. 1885. **100** Heinrich Handwerck 1928. **101** C.M. Bergmann 1910.

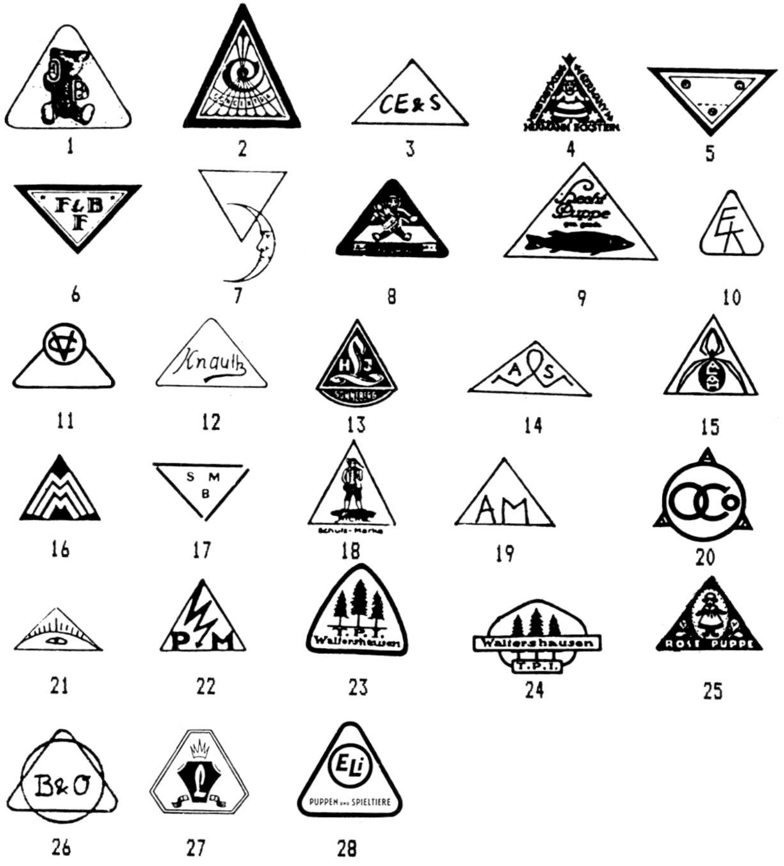

1 Oskar Büchner. **2** Concentra. **3** Christian Eichhorn & Söhne. **4** Hermann Eckstein. **5** Fleischmann & Bloedel 1895. **6** Fleischmann & Bloedel at the end of 1920'. **7** F. W. Goebel. **8** Carl Harmus 1905. **9** Else L. Hecht. **10** Erich Klötzer. **11** Kloster Veilsdorf. **12** Guido Knauth. **13** H. J. Leven. **14** Limbach AG. **15** Anni Lonz 1924. **16** Ma. E. Maar. **17** Sigismund Markmann. **18** Amandus Michaelis 1911. **19** Amandus Michaelis. **20** H. Offenbacher & Co. **21** Gebr. Ohlhaver (→ Porzellanfabrik Mengersgereuth). **22** Porzellanfabrik Mengersgereuth. **23+24** Thüringer Puppen-Industrie 1923. **25** F. Welsch 1925. **26** Brückner & Och. **27** H. Leh. **28** Ernst Liebermann.

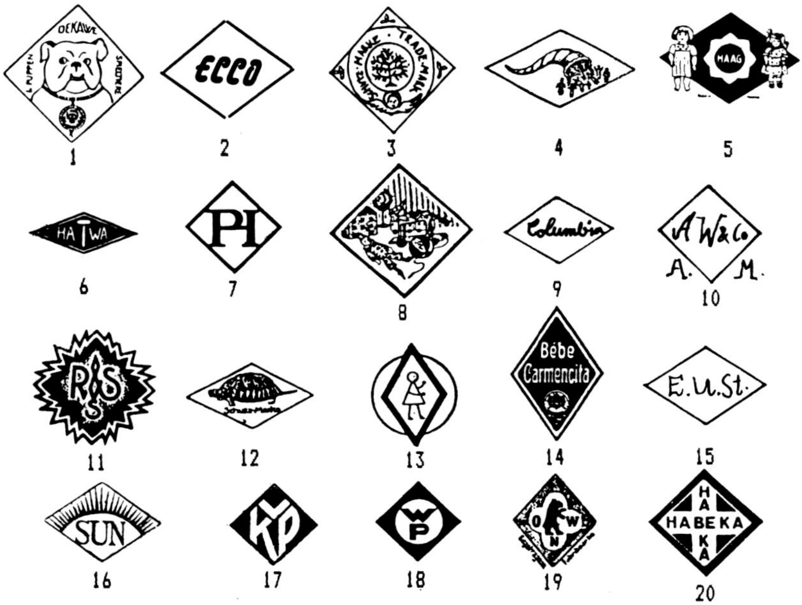

1 Deutsche Kolonial-Kapok-Werke 1925. 2 Hermann Eckstein. 3 A. Fleischmann Craemer 1881. 4 Carl Geyer & Co. 1900. 5 Gebr. Haag after 1920. 6 Hammer Munitionswerk 1920. 7 Dr. Paul Hunaeus 1901. 8 Richard Leutheuser. 9 Armand Marseille for C. M. Bergmann 1904. 10 Armand Marseille. 11 Rauch & Schelhorn. 12 Rheinische Gummi- and Celluloidwaren-Fabrik ca. 1909. 13 A. Riedeler. 14 Arthur Schoenau 1913. 15 E. U. Steiner. 16 Sigismund Ullmann 1922. 17 Vereinigte Köppelsdorfer Porzellanfabriken. 18 Waltershäuser Puppenfabrik 1921. 19 Otto Wohlmann 1908. 20 Hermann von Berg, 30' years.

1 Edgard Goldstein & Co. 1919. 2 Hahn & Co. 1921. 3 Max Handwerck 1901. 4 Carl Hartmann 1898. 5 Friedrich A. Heubach Nachf. 1920. 6 Werner Krauth 1920. 7 Louis Lindner & Söhne. 8 Karl Pietsch.

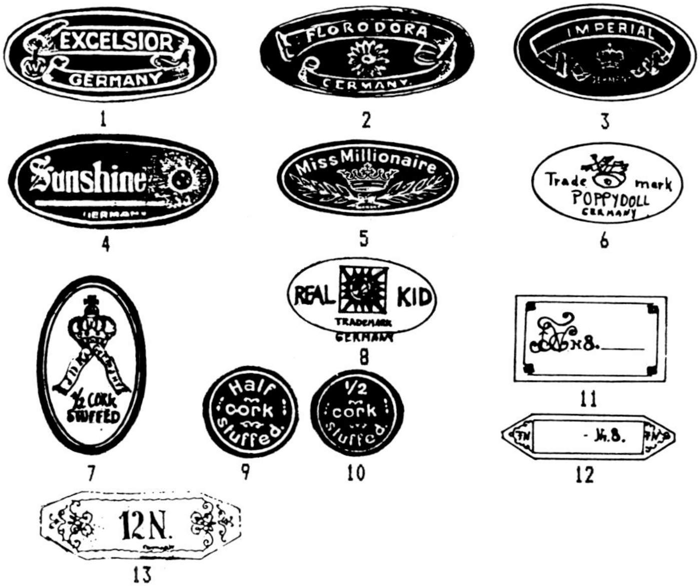

1 Louis Wolf & Co. **2** Geo. Borgfeldt & Co. 1903, with "Real Hair Eyesbows" 1910. **3** Hamburger & Co. 1901. **4** Sears, Roebuch & Co., made by an unknown firm. **5** Butler Brothers GmbH. 1913 (also used with "Non Plus Ultra"). **6** Cuno & Otto Dressel 1912. 7 J. D. Kestner jr. **8** Unknown. **9+10** Label made by different firms "Cork- or Hair-Stuffed" **11+12** Fischer, Naumann & Co. **13** Wagner & Zetsche.

1 F & W.Goebel. **2** Heber & Co. **3** J.D. Kestner jr. 1915. **4** J. D. Kestner jr. 1896. **5** Königl. Porzellanmanufaktur Berlin used since 1832. **6** Königl. Porzellanmanufaktur, used since 1837. **7** Edmund Knoch. **8** Limbach AG. **9** Andreas Müller 1896. **10** Schäfer & Vater. **11** Walther & Sohn. **12** Karl Standfuss.

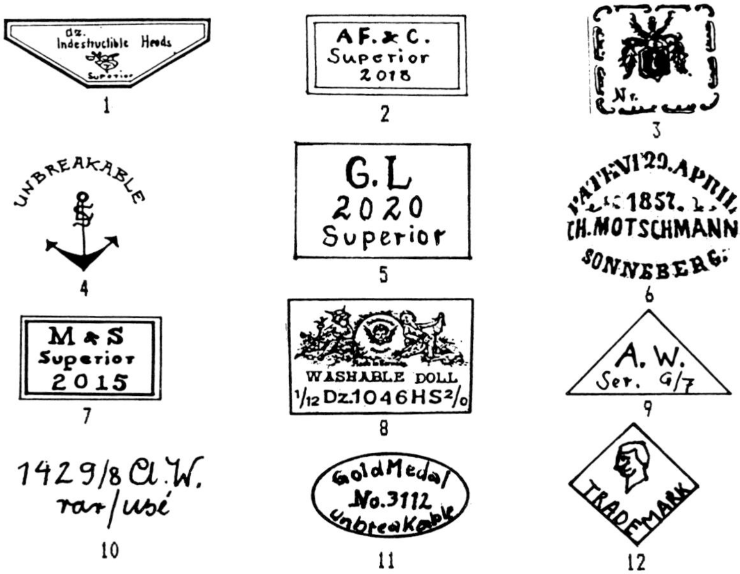

1 Cuno & Otto Dressel. 2 A. Fleischmann & Craemer. 3 Samuel Krauß 1875 (only found on figurines made of papermâché). 4 Lambert & Samhammer 1870. 5 Georg Lutz ca. 1887. 6 Christoph Motschmann 1857. 7 Müller & Strasburger. 8 F. M. Schilling 1879. 9+10 Adolf Wislizenus. 11+12 Unknown (only found on heads – with molded hairs – made of papermâché).

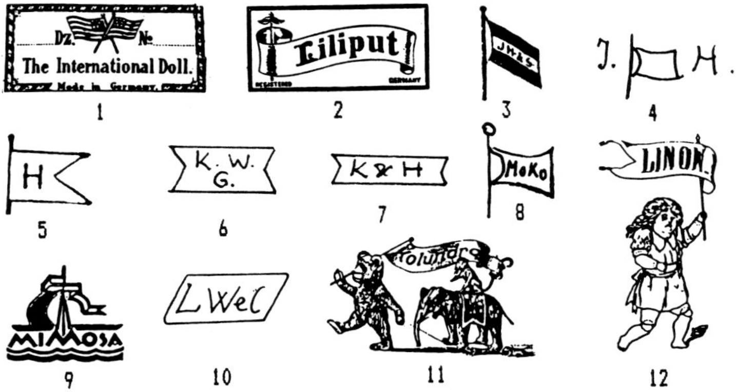

1 Geo. Borgfeldt & Co. 2 Carl Geyer 1902. 3+4 Hering & Sohn. 5 Ernst Heubach. 6 Keramisches Werk Gräfenhain. 7 Kley & Hahn. 8 M. Kohnstamm & Co. 9 Mimosa 1923. 10 Louis Wolf & Co. 11 Kohler & Rosenwald 1927. 12 Hermann Landshut & Co. 1895.

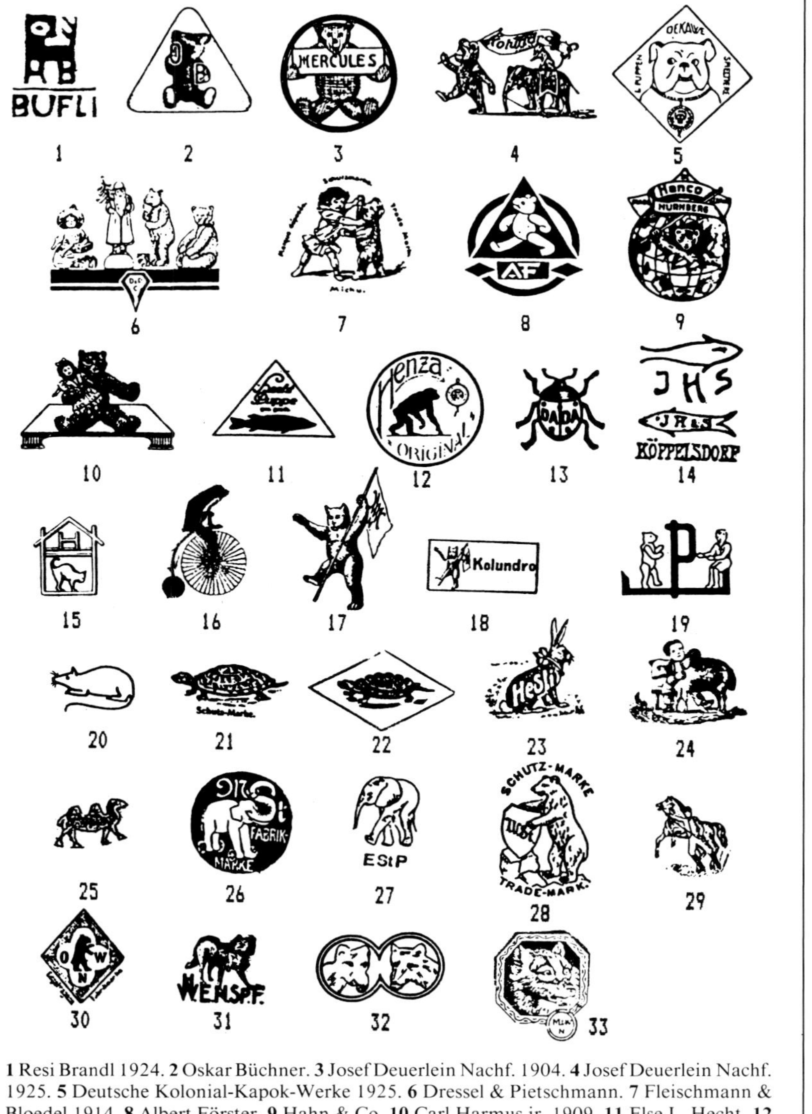

1 Resi Brandl 1924. **2** Oskar Büchner. **3** Josef Deuerlein Nachf. 1904. **4** Josef Deuerlein Nachf. 1925. **5** Deutsche Kolonial-Kapok-Werke 1925. **6** Dressel & Pietschmann. **7** Fleischmann & Bloedel 1914. **8** Albert Förster. **9** Hahn & Co. **10** Carl Harmus jr. 1909. **11** Else L. Hecht. **12** Henze & Steinhäuser 1925. **13** Hermsdorfer Celluloidwarenfabrik. **14** Hering & Sohn. **15** Hertwig & Co. **16** Hugo Heubach. **17** Martin Winterbauer. **18** Kohler & Rosenwald. **19** Louis Philipp Luthardt. **20** Edith Maus 1925. **21+22** Rheinische Gummi- and Celluloid-Fabrik used since 1899 in various kind. **23** Heinrich Schmuckler 1921. **24** Wilhelm Simon 1875. **25** Margarete Steiff ca. 1892. **26** Margarete Steiff ca. 1898. **27** Erste Steinbacher Porzellanfabrik. **28** Wilhelm Strunz. **29** Heinrich Weiß 1895. **30** Otto Wohlmann 1908. **31** Hermann Wolf 1923. **32** Gebr. Wolff. **33** Maienthal & Wolff, 1925.

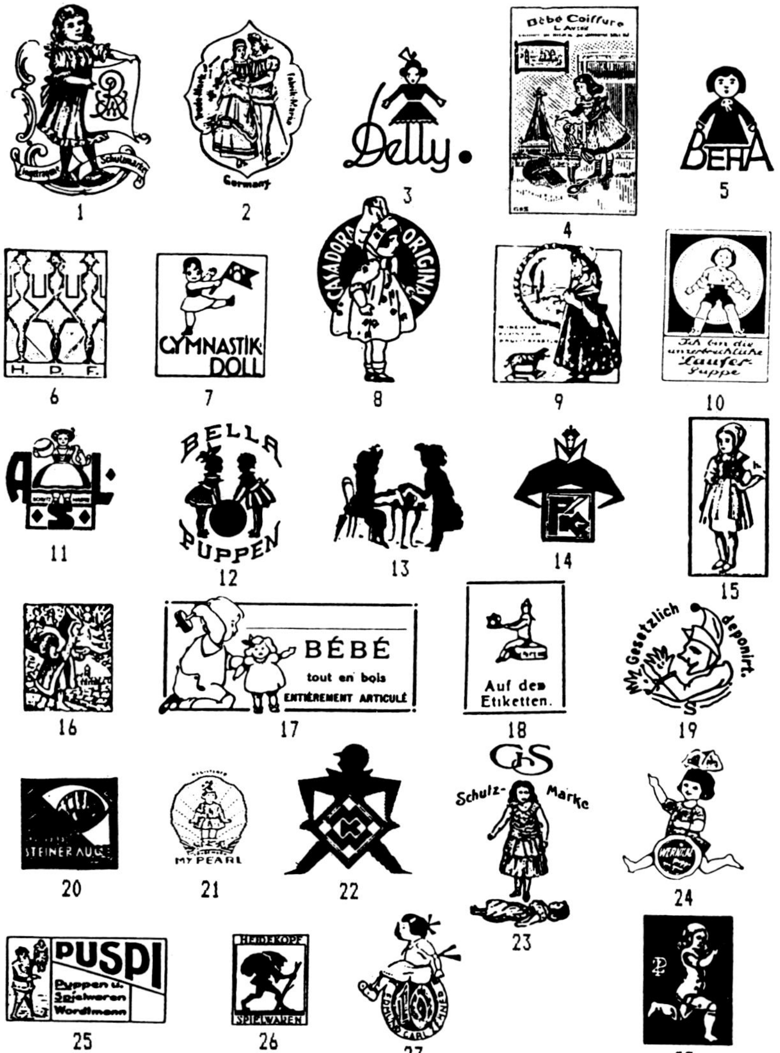

1 Richard Beck & Co. 1903. **2** Johannes Franz 1858. **3** Delly Puppenfabrik 1925. **4** Gutmann & Schiffnie 1911. **5** Berthold Helk 1927. **6** Herzpuppen-Fabrik 1923. **7** Albin Heß 1930. **8** Huttinger & Buschow 1921. **9** Marion Kaulitz 1909. **10** Arthur Laufer 1925. **11** Anton Link 1924. **12** Leo Nordschild 1924. **13** Gebr. Paris 1907. **14** Puppen-Industrie Gotha 1924. **15** Rotkäppchen GmbH. 1925. **16** Richard Scherzer 1924. **17** Rudolf Schneider 1914. **18** Simon & Halbig 1875. **19** Max Spindler. **20** Hermann Steiner, Neustadt 1927. **21** Hermann Steiner, Sonneberg. **22** Josef Strasser 1922. **23** Gebr. Süssenguth 1909 and Gutmann & Schiffnie 1907. **24** Paul Wernicke 1925. **25** H. Wordtmann 1925. **26** Württembergische Spielwarenfabrik 1924. **27** Edmund Carl Zehner 1924. **28** P.R. Zierow 1910.

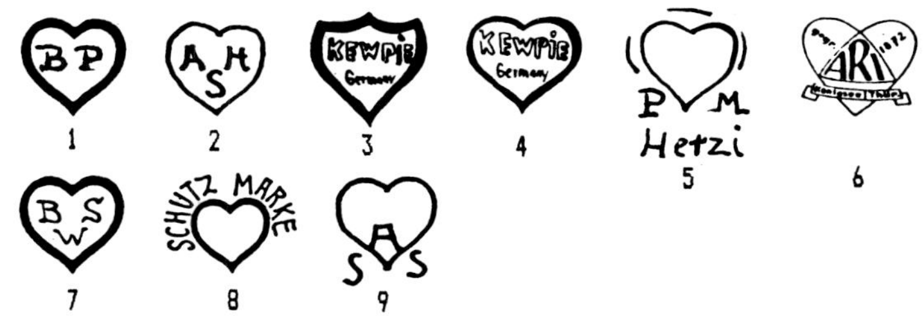

1 Baehr & Proeschild. 2 Albin Heß. 3+4 Labels for Kewpies. 5 Porzellanfabrik Mengersgereuth. 6 A. Riedeler. 7+8 Bruno Schmidt 9 Arthur Schoenau.

1 Bühl & Söhne. 2 Kloster Veilsdorf. 3–5 Limbach AG. 6 Hermann Pensky. 7 Adolf Wislizenus.

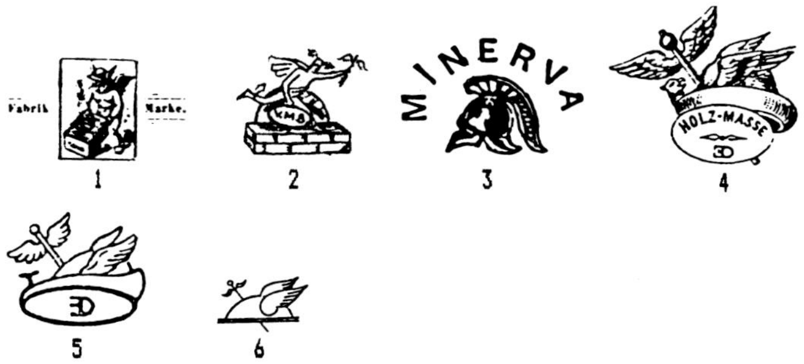

1 Max Oscar Arnold. 2 V.M.Bruchlos. 3 Buschow & Beck 1900. 4+5+6 Cuno & Otto Dressel.

1 Max Oscar Arnold. **2** Curnen & Steiner 1898. **3** Otto Schamberger. **4** Theodor Wendt 1924.

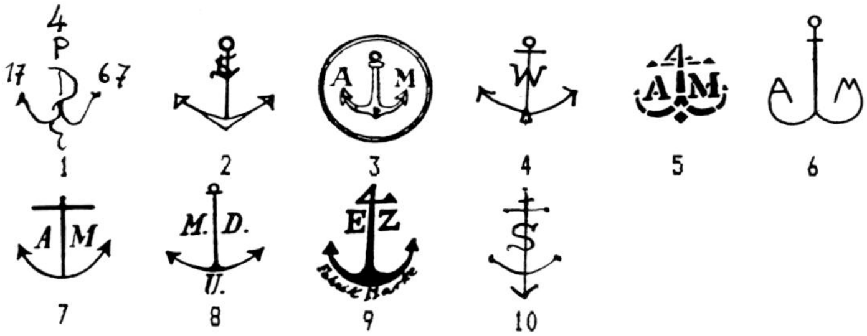

1 Johann Philipp Dressel. **2** Lambert & Samhammer 1876. **3** Armand Marseille, ca. 1893. **4** Armand Marseille for Louis Wolf & Co. 1896. **5** Armand Marseille, ca. 1910. **6** Armand Marseille 1910. **7** Armand Marseille 1920. **8** Möller & Dippe. **9** Emil Zitzmann 1913. **10** Philipp Samhammer.

1 Gebr. Metzler & Ortloff. **2+3** Theodor Recknagel. **4+5+6+7+8** various trademarks of Franz Schmidt & Co.

1 Emil Bauersachs. **2** A. Fleischmann & Craemer. **3** Porzellanfabrik Mengersgereuth 1908. **4+5** Gebr. Heubach. **6** Carl A.Illing & Co. **7** Gebr. Kühnlenz. **8** A. Luge & Co. 1926. **9** Heinrich Liebermann 1927. **10** Morgenroth & Co. **11** W. G. Müller. **12** Müller & Fröbel. **13** Gebr. Ohlhaver. **14** Preussig & Wilson 1914. **15** Paul Schmidt 1923. **16** Seyfarth & Reinhardt 1923. **17** Sigismund Ullmann 1926. **18** Friedrich Voigt. **19** Welsch & Co. **20+21** Eduard Fleischmann & Söhne, 1893.

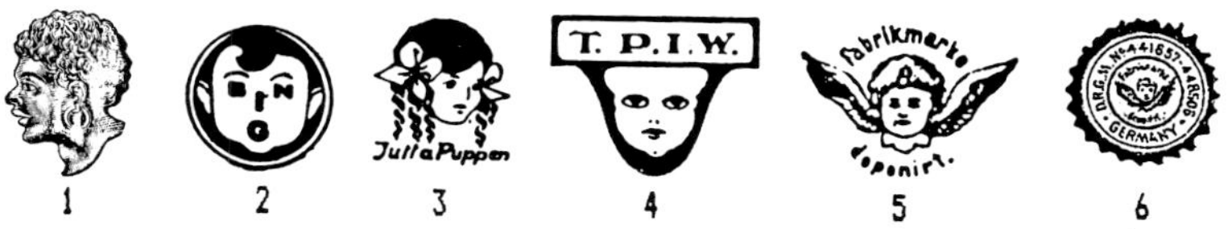

1 L. Bierer 1908. **2** Bing Künstlerpuppen- and Stoffspielwarengesellschaft. **3** Cuno & Otto Dressel 1907. **4** Thüringer Puppenindustrie 1923. **5** F. M. Schilling, 1883. **6** F. M. Schilling 1910.

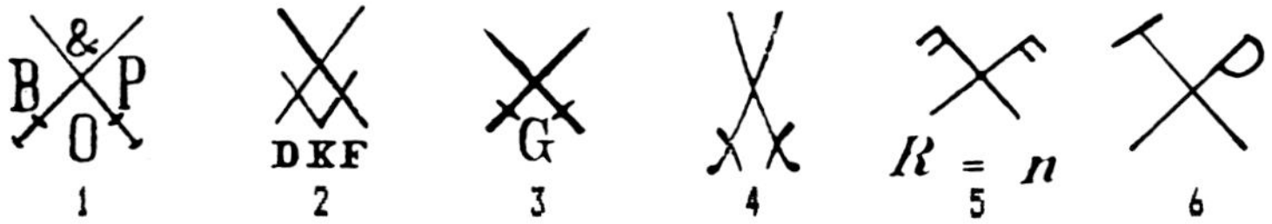

1 Baehr & Proeschild. **2** Dornheim, Koch & Fischer. **3** Theodor Degenring. **4** Königl. Porzellanmanufaktur Meissen. **5** Porzellanfabrik Rauenstein. **6** Theodor Pohl, Böhmen.

1+2 Ernst Heubach. **3** Johannes Franz 1892. **4** Alfred Heller 1903. **5** E. Escher jun. 1896.

1 Cellba Celluloidwarenfabrik. **2** Conta & Böhme. **3** Berthold Eck 1876. **4** Otto Gans. **5** Gebr. Heubach. **6** Hermann Heyde 1910. **7** Königl. Bayer. Porzellan-Manufaktur. **8** Samuel Krauß 1875. **9** Sonneberger Porzellanfabrik Carl Müller. **10** Theodor Recknagel. **11** Max Friedrich Schellhorn 1908. **12** Arthur Schoenau. **13** Unger & Schilde. **14** Zeuch & Lausmann 1895. **15** Sonneberger Wappen. **16** Louis Roth, 1893.

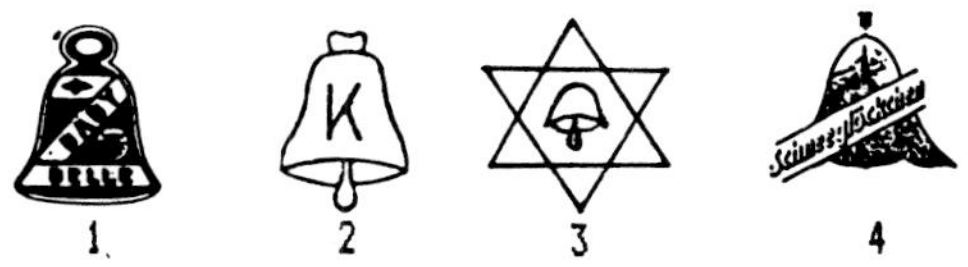

1 Geo. Borgfeldt & Co. 1908. **2** C.F. Kling. **3** presumable C.F. Kling for K&R. **4** Nöckler & Tittel.

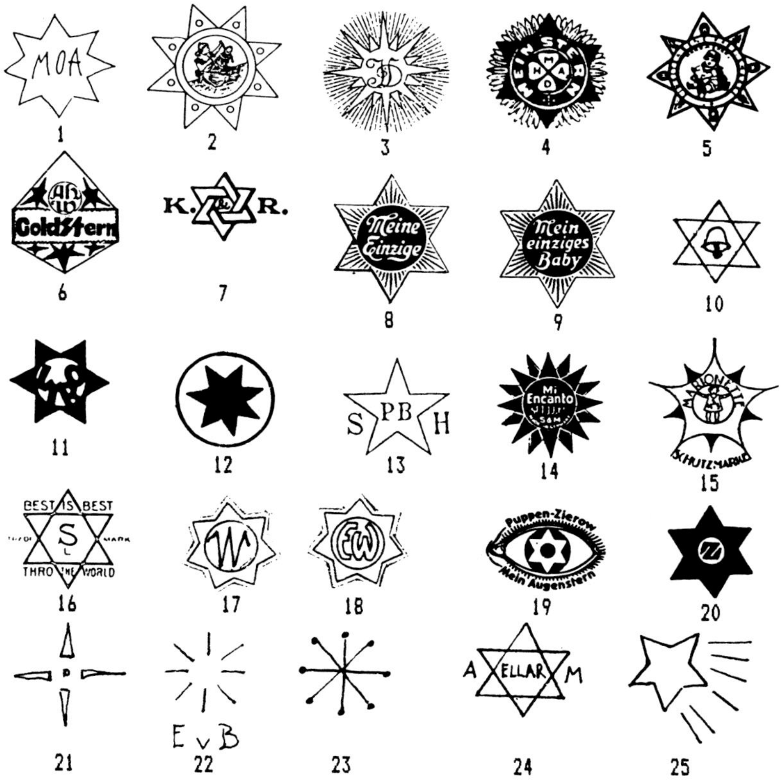

1 Max Oscar Arnold. **2** C. M. Bergmann ca. 1926. **3** Julius Dorst 1895. **4** Henriette Dunker 1923. **5** Heinrich Handwerck 1891 (used on trademark "Bebe Cosmopolite" and "Bebe de Reclame". **6** Adolf Hülß 1925. **7** Kämmer & Reinhardt 1896. **8** Kley & Hahn 1910. **9** Kley & Hahn 1913. **10** presumable C. F. Kling for K&R. **11** Lyro-Puppen-Company 1923 and Rolfes & Co. 1923. **12** Moritz Pappe 1907. **13** Schoenau & Hoffmeister. **14** Seligmann & Mayer 1930. **15** Mylius Sperschneider 1922. **16** Josef Süsskind. **17** Ernst Winkler 1910. **18** Ernst Winkler 1925. **19** P. R. Zierow 1914. **20** Gottlieb Zinner & Söhne. **21** Cuno & Otto Dressel. **22** Erich von Berg. **23** unknown. **24** Armand Marseille. Note: C. M. Bergmann and Adolf Hülß both used around 1925 „Mein Goldstern". **25** August Möller & Sohn, 1925.

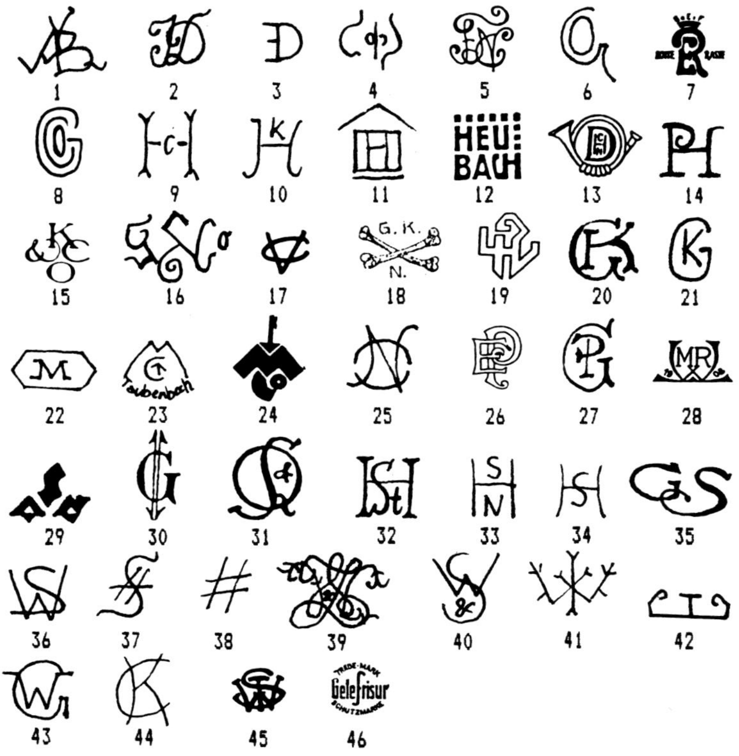

1 Alt, Beck & Gottschalck. 2 Julius Dorst. 3+4 Cuno & Otto Dressel. 5 Fischer, Naumann & Co. 6 Otto Gans. 7 Greif-Puppenkunst. 8 Greiner & Co. 9 Heber & Co. 10 Carl Hartmann. 11 Hertwig & Co. 12 Gebr. Heubach. 13 Carl Horn Nachf. 14 Dr. Paul Huneaus. 15+16 Kestner & Comp. 17 Kloster Veilsdorf. 18 Gebr. Knoch. 19 Kohl & Wengenroth. 20 Gustav Korn. 21 Gebr. Kühnlenz. 22 Marienfeld. 23 Carl Moritz. 24 Karl Müller & Co. 25 Nikolaus Oberender. 26 Emil Pfeifer. 27 Fritz Pfeiffer. 28 Max Rudolph. 29 August Schellhorn. 30 Carl Schneider Erben. 31 Schützmeister & Quendt. 32+33+34 Hermann Steiner. 35 Gebr. Süssenguth. 36 Strobel & Wilken. 37+38 Gebr. Voigt (38 = see Alt, Beck & Gottschalck). 39 Wagner & Zetsche. 40 Walther & Sohn. 41 Johann Walter. 42 presumable Theodor Wendt. 43 Gustav Wohlleben. 44 Carl Knoll, Böhmen. 45 Weiskirchner Steingutfabrik, Böhmen. 46 Gustav Thiele.

1 2 3 4 5

1 Emil Bauersachs 1895. 2 Fleischmann & Bloedel 1890. 3 Dr. Paul Huneaus. 4 Johann Heinrich Kletzin & Co. 5 Nöckler & Tittel.

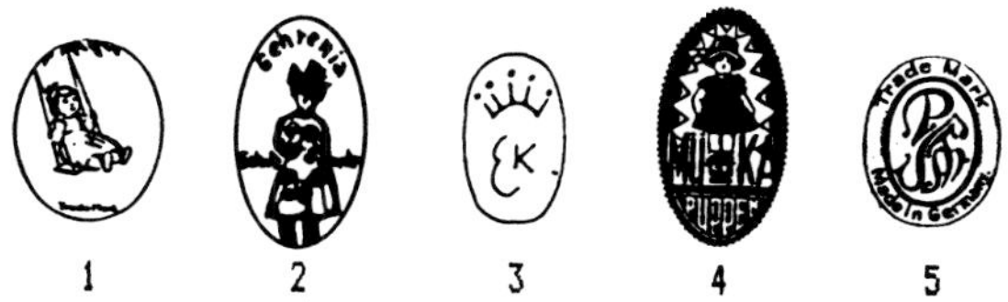

1 Max Göhring 1924. **2** Henze & Steinhäuser 1912. **3** Edmund Knoch. **4** Müller & Kaltwasser. **5** Paul Schmidt 1922.

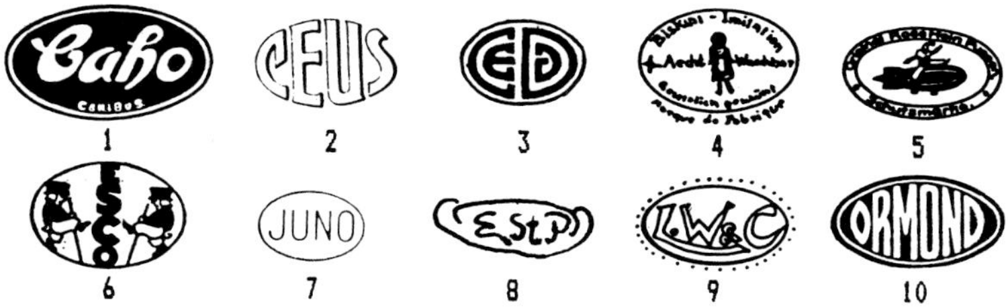

1 Canzler & Hoffmann 1925. **2** Christian Eichhorn & Söhne. **3** C. Erich Günther 1922. **4** Gebr. Haag 1886. **5** Therese Heininger 1925. **6** Sommer & Co. GmbH. 7 Karl Standfuss. **8** Erste Steinbacher Porzellanfabrik. **9** Louis Wolf & Co. **10** D. H. Wagner & Sohn, 1928.

1 Otto Gans. **2** Paul Hausmeister & Co. **3** Jacob Jung 1912. **4+5** August Luge & Co. **6** Schwäbische Celluloidwaren-Fabrik. **7** Emil Schwenk. **8** Sigismund Schwerin Nachf. 1923. **9+10** Reich, Goldmann & Co., Offenbacher Celluloidwarenfabrik. **11** „Ulmer Spatz", Württembergische Puppenwerkstätte, 1926. **12** Robert Hiller 1890.